1648 AND ALL THAT

The Scottish Invasions of England, 1648 and 1651. Proceedings of the 2022 Helion and Company 'Century of the Soldier' Conference

Edited by Charles Singleton

Helion & Company Limited

Helion & Company Limited
Unit 8 Amherst Business Centre
Budbrooke Road
Warwick
CV34 5WE
England
Tel. 01926 499 619
Email: info@helion.co.uk
Website: www.helion.co.uk
Twitter: @helionbooks
Visit our blog http://blog.helion.co.uk/

Published by Helion & Company 2023
Designed and typeset by Mary Woolley, Battlefield Design
Cover designed by Paul Hewitt, Battlefield Design (www.battlefield-design.co.uk)

Text © as individually credited 2023
Illustrations © as individually credited

Every reasonable effort has been made to trace copyright holders and to obtain their permission for the use of copyright material. The author and publisher apologize for any errors or omissions in this work, and would be grateful if notified of any corrections that should be incorporated in future reprints or editions of this book.

ISBN 978-1-804513-64-4

British Library Cataloguing-in-Publication Data.
A catalogue record for this book is available from the British Library.

All rights reserved. No part of this publication may be reproduced, stored in a retrieval system, or transmitted, in any form, or by any means, electronic, mechanical, photocopying, recording or otherwise, without the express written consent of Helion & Company Limited.

For details of other military history titles published by Helion & Company Limited, contact the above address, or visit our website: http://www.helion.co.uk

We always welcome receiving book proposals from prospective authors.

Contents

List of Contributors iv
Introduction vi
Foreword by Ronald Hutton vii

Colonel Francis Thornhagh, Oliver Cromwell and the Battle of Preston, 1648
   Stuart B. Jennings 9
A Tale of Two Risings
   Peter Gaunt 21
Three Armies into One? Scottish Engager Military Organisation in 1648
   Edward M. Furgol 40
The Control of Command in the British Wars 1642–1651
   Malcolm Wanklyn 47
"For Suppressing Any Forraigne Invasion, Intestine Trouble or Insurrection"
Fortress Scotland – 1650–1707 from the 2019 National Army Museum conference
   David Flintham 74
Logistics of Rebellion 1685 from the 2019 National Army Museum conference
   Stephen Carter 101

List of Contributors

Ronald Hutton
Ronald Hutton is a leading authority on history of the British Isles in the sixteenth and seventeenth centuries, as well as on ancient and medieval paganism and magic, and on the global context of witchcraft beliefs. He is the author of the definitive *The Pagans: A History* as well as *The Rise and Fall of Merrie England*, *The Restoration* and a biography of Charles II. He frequently appears as an expert on TV and radio.

Peter Gaunt
Peter Gaunt is Professor of Early Modern History at the University of Chester. A past chairman and current president of The Cromwell Association, he has written and published extensively on the military and wider history of the civil wars in Wales, England and Britain as a whole, on Oliver Cromwell as soldier, politician and statesman and on the political history of the Cromwellian Protectorate. The author or editor of 16 books and well over 60 articles, chapters and short papers, most recently he revised and prepared a new edition of Barry Coward's *The Stuart Age*, published by Routledge in February 2017, and is working on a full-length study of the personal experiences of war, as reflected in surviving first personal accounts, to be published by Helion.

Stuart B. Jennings
Dr Stuart B. Jennings is an Early Modern historian and a retired University chaplain. He continues to lecture at the Centre for Lifelong Learning, University of Warwick, where he has been teaching for the last 12 years. He has published numerous peer-reviewed articles on the seventeenth century and the British Civil Wars and has written two books and contributed chapters to two others on the seventeenth century. His book *'These Uncertaine Tymes': Newark and the Civilian Experience of the English Civil Wars, 1640–1660* was a winner of the 2010 Alan Ball Prize for Local History

Edward Furgol
Having completed a D.Phil in Modern History in 1982, Furgol became a curator for the Pendle Heritage Centre in Lancashire, Northern England. His next post was with Historic Scotland. Moving back to the United States in 1987, he worked at the National Museum of the United States Navy, until

he retired as managing director in 2017. He published the first edition of *The Regimental History of the Covenanting Armies 1639–1651* in 1990.

Malcolm Wanklyn
Professor Wanklyn studied the English Civil War at the University of Manchester. He then joined the staff of what later became the University of Wolverhampton where he completed his doctorate on allegiance in Cheshire and Shropshire in 1642, and taught courses on Early Modern England and Regional History. He also served for 10 years as head of History. On retiring in 2002 he returned to his first love, and since then has written six books on the British Wars, most notably *Decisive Battles of English Civil War* (2006) and *Parliament's Generals* (2019)

David Flintham
David Flintham is a military historian specialising in the fortress warfare of the so-called 'English' Civil Wars. He is the co-founder and project director of the King's Lynn under Siege community archaeology project, and is also part of a research project 're-discovering' London's ECW fortifications. He is currently developing a register identifying and listing every ECW-period fortification throughout Britain and Ireland. The author of three books, and nearly 70 other papers, in 2022, he organised the ECW fortress symposium, the first-ever such event dedicated to the study of the period's fortresses and sieges. A long-time member of the Fortress Study Group, he serves on its committee.

Stephen Carter
Stephen Carter has spent the last 25 years researching the Life and Times of the Duke of Monmouth and the Whig movement. For his first book, Fighting for Liberty, he has returned to original sources to give a fresh and vibrant account of the military campaign of 1685. Stephen juggles working full-time with writing, living in France, and publishing his findings on Twitter as @Warwalks.

Introduction

The annual Century of the Soldier conference returned after a hiatus of two years due to the global Covid-19 Pandemic in May 2022. The returning conference was held in the new venue of Worcester Cathedral's Undercroft.

The obvious theme for the conference was the Scottish invasions of England in 1648 and 1651. Not only did Worcester witness the last major battle of the British Civil Wars, but the Cathedral was used as a temporary prison to hold the Scottish prisoners. The title of the Conference, '1648 and all that' was a nod towards the famous 1930 book by W.C. Sellar and R.J. Yeatman '1066 and all that'. The conference was very well attended, and we were fortunate to have papers by the leading lights of British Civil War. The venue lent itself well to the event and it was also the first time we were able to use video conferencing facilities to host papers by Professor Malcolm Wanklyn speaking from Wolverhampton and Edward Furgol who gave his paper from his home on the east coast of the United States.

The publication of the 2022 conference proceedings has also given us the opportunity to include some of the papers from the 2019 conference that was run at the National Army Museum. Unfortunately, due to disruption caused by the pandemic, we were unable to publish the proceedings of the 2019 conference, so we hope to make amends with publishing two of the papers in this book.

The conference was a great success and we received a lot of very positive feedback from those that attended. As I write this foreword, I am looking forward to the 2023 conference.

I'd like to thank the delegates for their attendance and to say thank you to the conference goers who, thanks to their support have not only made the event the lead in the field, but given their ongoing support of the Century of the Soldier book series.

Charles Singleton
Creative Director Antiquity and Early Modern Portfolio, Helion and Company

Foreword

Ronald Hutton

The period between the years 1647 and 1651 generally gets a bad press in every part of the British Isles. In England its military events are put under the labels of the Second and Third Civil Wars, viewed as mere postscripts to the real English Civil War, the 'great' one of 1642 to 1646, which was decisive for the future of the nation and provided historical memory with the emblematic figures of the Roundhead and Cavalier. It has been said that Dame Veronica Wedgewood abandoned her intention of continuing her celebrated history of the civil wars of the 1640s beyond 1646, because the following years seemed mostly too tedious and too complex to make a gripping narrative. The English Revolution of 1649 does remain a charismatic and divisive event, but an isolated and brief one, and to the Scots and Irish the military operations between 1649 and 1651 represent nadirs in both their histories, traumatic and humiliating episodes which embodied the definitive English conquest of each country. Modern English people, however, do not remember them with any sense of glory either, as the annexation of those other nations into an English republican empire proved short-lived, and this makes the slaughters that accompanied their conquest seem even more regrettable. As for England itself, not much seems to survive in popular memory from the warfare of 1648 and 1651 except a vague memory of a couple of big battles, and the closing image of a king in an oak tree.

All this is not historically just, because English military affairs in 1648 and 1651 were in several respects as important, and even more decisive, than those of the earlier 1640s. They were part of a truly international conflict, spanning all three kingdoms, and their consequences were profound, and lasting. They included some of the biggest battles in British history, those usually given the name of Preston and Worcester. Both were highly unusual in that neither was a set-piece action in open country between formed armies. One was a three-day running fight across most of a county, and the other an assault on a fortified city, without prior bombardment or mining, as if it had been an enemy in the open field. Both conflicts tore up the pattern of loyalties found in the earlier civil war, comrades from the latter now finding themselves fighting on opposite sides. Their short-term positive and negative effects were profound. On the positive side, they established Oliver Cromwell as the leading military and political figure in the British Isles, in prime position to become, a few years later, the only commoner in British history to become a head of state. They also determined that religious pluralism would become the norm in all three nations, instead of each having an intolerant and comprehensive established Church. On the negative, and equally significant, side of the historical ledger, they finally ruined both the Scottish Covenanter cause of 1639–40 and the English Parliamentarian one of 1642. Both had been devoted to the establishment of monopolistic national presbyterian Churches, and a constitutional monarchy firmly limited by Parliaments and underpinned by an enduring Anglo-Scottish alliance, as a partnership between equals. Their vision had appeared victorious in the mid-1640s, but was utterly destroyed by those two battles.

The long-term consequences were just as important, and easy to track. One was to make England the dominant nation in the British Isles, leaving Ireland and Scotland the alternatives of engaging as junior partners in a superpower formed under English leadership or resisting and being subjected to further military defeat and reprisal. The former outcome was to prevail and establish the context for the emergence of the British Empire and Industrial Revolution. The conflicts of 1648–51 imposed a Protestant Ascendancy upon Ireland, turning the majority of the population into a subaltern class for almost another 300 years. They also destroyed Scottish confidence in national independence, leading first to a new loyalism towards the Stuart monarchy, and then to a political union with England that (however shakily) endures to the present day. They turned English monarchs from a flirtation with Presbyterianism and the English landed elite from one with populism against the Crown. Instead they resulted in a solid alliance between Crown, episcopal Church and hereditary nobility that was to last for 200 years and substantially survives today.

The imposition of religious pluralism ensured the continued existence of radical Protestant groups such as Presbyterians, congregational independents and Baptists, who were to endure to the present time, and allowed the appearance of others, notably Quakers. When tolerance of these was withdrawn in the 1660s, they were too strongly established to be extirpated, and freedom of conscience had rapidly to be restored to them. The result was the creation of one of the world's most diverse and dynamic national cultures, allowing and encouraging an astonishing richness of debate and creativity in all spheres of intellectual, literary and artistic endeavour. The huge contribution of Dissent to Victorian Britain was made possible by the outcome of the fighting of these years. In addition, the effect of the military victories of English radicals in these years was to hold apart the divisions inflicted on traditional society by the previous civil war in the political as well as the military sphere. Victory in either 1648 or 1651 for the alliances between English Royalists and Parliamentarians and Scottish Covenanters which were decisively defeated in those years, would probably have healed the partisan fractures of the earlier conflict. Instead the radical triumph deepened and embittered division until it became entrenched, and English politics have been framed by a two-party system ever since. Royalists and Parliamentarians evolved into Whigs and Tories, and then into Liberals and Conservatives, and so into Socialists and Conservatives, and the pattern is still sustained.

Finally, the wars studied here, and the military actions in Scotland and Ireland to which they were intrinsically linked, gave a vital boost to England's Caribbean colonies, sending them around 10,000 extra plantation workers in the shape of prisoners of war. That economic shot in the arm, reinforced by Cromwell's conquest of Jamaica in 1655 – itself an outgrowth of the programme established by his victorious army – started the process by which these island possessions became the richest part of the empire by the eighteenth century and gave a vital push to England's urbanisation and industrialisation. The expansion of plantation agriculture that these enforced workers enabled, also created a demand for labour which after the supply of prisoners dried up could only be satisfied by enslaved Africans. That in turn set in train a sequence of events contributing substantially to the remarkable ethnic and cultural diversity of contemporary British society.

A case could credibly be made, therefore, that it was the relatively despised and neglected Second and Third Civil Wars, and the Scottish invasions of England which lay at their core, that created modern Britain. It is also the more important and delightful, therefore, that Helion has provided us with such a large and exciting edition of essays upon them. The list of contributors includes established and influential academics, talented newcomers to the university system, and respected independent scholars. Together, they make a significant contribution towards an understanding of conflicts that have done so much to fashion our world.

Colonel Francis Thornhagh, Oliver Cromwell and the Battle of Preston, 1648

Stuart B. Jennings

Introduction

Following the successful defeat of a combined army consisting of Scots under the command of the Duke of Hamilton and Royalists under Marmaduke Langdale at Preston in 1648, the commander of the victorious Parliamentarian army wrote to the Speaker of the House of Commons. In this, Oliver Cromwell gave a full account of the battle and concluded it with a more personal comment about one of his senior officers.

> I ordered Colonel Thorhagh to command two or three regiments of horse to follow the enemy, if it were possible to make him stand still till we could bring up the army. The enemy marched away 7000 or 8000 foot and about 4000 horse, we followed him with about 3000 foot and 2500 horse and dragoons; ad in this prosecution that worthy gentleman Colonel Thornhagh, pressing too boldly, was slain, being run into the body, and thigh, and head by the enemy's launcers: and give me leave to say he was a man as faithful and gallant in your service as any, and one who often heretofore lost blood in your quarrel, and now his last. He hath left some behind to inherit a father's honour,a nd a grieving widow – both now in the interest of the commonwealth.[1]

Cromwell speaks with great affection and respect for Thornhagh. This was not just a fellow officer but also someone who was known to Cromwell, who had served alongside him and more recently under his direct command in Wales at the start of the Second Civil War. Thornhagh was also well known in the Commons where he had served as an active MP, sitting on a several committees since his election in 1646 for the Nottinghamshire town of Retford. Such was Cromwell's growing regard for Thornhagh's military skills that he gave him a battlefield promotion to take charge of three regiments of horse to pursue the fleeing Scots and slow them down. This would enable Cromwell and his infantry to catch up and finish the task of defeating them completely.

---

1   S. C. Lomas (ed.), *The Letters and Speeches of Oliver Cromwell with Elucidations by Thomas Carlyle*, 3 vols (London: Methuen & Co, 1904), I. pp.279–85.

This chapter seeks to explore the rise of Colonel Thornhagh, his growing support not only for the parliament but also the army cause and his evolving relationship with Cromwell that eventually led to Thornhagh's role at the battle of Preston.

The Making of Francis Thornhagh

Who was this Francis Thornhagh who arrived alongside Cromwell to the Battle at Preston? What follows is not a full biography but rather a spotlight on key elements that made him who he was and drew him into the orbit of Cromwell's attention.[2]

Born in 1617, Francis was the oldest surviving son of Sir Francis Thornhagh and his wife Jane. Francis Thornhagh received the standard education bestowed on the heir of a gentry's family – Grammar School, University and finally a brief period at one of the Inns of Court. The Thornhagh family were a rising gentry family within Nottinghamshire, with Sir Francis serving as both a JP and High Sheriff of Nottingham (1637–1638). In the latter role he found himself caught up in contentious issues such as the drainage of the Isle of Axholme and the raising of Ship Money. These experiences probably contributed to Sir Francis and his son Francis developing political sympathies that eventually led them to side with parliament in 1642.

It was during his early years that Francis developed both his religious sympathies and formed a number of lasting friendships. The parish of Sturton le Steeple in north Nottinghamshire, where the family resided, had a long and turbulent history of Puritanism. The separatist leaders John Robinson and John Smith were both born and raised in the parish and until their exile overseas preached in and around the parish. Though there is no surviving evidence to directly link the Thornhagh family with separatism, they do appear not to have been unsympathetic to Puritanism.[3] Later during the 1640s and 1650s, the Nottinghamshire horse was increasingly identified with the toleration of religious thought and dissent whilst under the command of Francis Thornhagh. It was also during his childhood that Francis developed both his love and knowledge of horses, an interest greatly encouraged by his father Sir Francis. During the Bishops' Wars of 1639–1640,

Full size life portrait of Colonel Francis Thornhagh c1640. Artist unknown (With thanks to G. M. T. Foljambe Esq. of Osberton for use of this image).

---

2   For a full biography see Stuart B. Jennings, *'A Very Gallant Gentleman': Colonel Francis Thornhagh (1617–1648) and the Nottinghamshire Horse*, (Warwick: Helion, 2022).
3   Stuart B. Jennings, *'The Gathering of the Elect': The Development, Nature and Socio–Economic Structures of Protestant Religious Dissent in Seventeenth Century Nottinghamshire* (Unpublished PhD Thesis, Nottingham Trent University, 1999), pp.31–100.

Sir Francis was appointed by parliament to identify and secure good quality horses within the shire for the use of the King's army, a task that his son Francis most certainly assisted him with. It was to put them both in good stead at the start of the English Civil War in 1642.

The other significant factor noted during his formative childhood years was the creation of a life-long friendship with John Hutchinson, formed during their time together at the Lincoln Free Grammar School. Lucy Hutchinson recorded in her *Memoirs* that at the school, where there were many gentlemen's sons, there was

> an old Low-country soldier [who] was entertained to train them in arms, and they all brought themselves weapons; and, instead of childish sports, when they were not at their books, were exercised in all their military postures, and in assaults and defences; which instruction was not useless in a few years after, to some of them; and Colonel Thornhagh, who was now trained in this sportive militia with Colonel Hutchinson, afterwards was his fellow soldier in earnest, when the great cause of God's and England's rights came to be disputed with swords against encroaching princes.[4]

This friendship was to further blossom in their shared military commitment to the Parliamentarian cause in Nottingham after 1642, with Hutchinson being appointed Governor of Nottingham Castle and Thornhagh being appointed Commander of the county's cavalry regiment. Their friendship and service together whilst in Nottinghamshire is recorded in great detail in the *Memoirs of Colonel John Hutchinson*, written by Lucy Hutchinson.

Towards the end of 1638, Francis Thornhagh went to the Netherlands to further develop his interest and knowledge of military matters. It was here he encountered the military innovations that had been developed by both Gustavus Adolphus and Maurice of Nassu over the course of the Thirty Years War. His love of horsemanship particularly attracted him to the Swedish model of the full cavalry charge into opponents without halting to discharge pistols. This meant that the troopers rode into their enemies at a velocity that would not have been possible if they had stopped to fire their pistols halfway through the charge. Thornhagh was to use this tactic in at least three of his battles in the first civil war.

Towards the end of 1642, Sir Francis Thornhagh was commissioned to raise a regiment of horse within Nottinghamshire for the service of Parliament.[5] This he undertook, but most of the work of raising and equipping the regiment he appeared to hand over to his son Francis, whom he appointed his second in command as a lieutenant colonel. One of Francis' first acts was to appoint his friend Henry Ireton, who had just returned from the battle of Edgehill, as the major of the new regiment. Ireton brought with him into the newly formed regiment his battle-experienced troop of horse. Together Francis and Henry Ireton quickly disciplined the newly formed regiment into an effective fighting unit. Sir Francis death in April 1643 saw Francis take command of the regiment and promoted to the rank of colonel. Thornhagh probably received his commission as colonel of the regiment from Lord Grey of Groby who was commander-in-chief of the Midland counties.[6] This command he retained up until his death in 1648.

Over the course of the first civil war Francis and his regiment saw extensive military service both across the Midlands and wider afield. On three occasions – Gainsborough (1643), Newark (1644) and Rowton Heath (1645) – Thornhagh led his regiment in a Swedish style charge on his opponents.

---

4 N. H. Keeble, *Lucy Hutchinson, Memoirs of the Life of Colonel Hutchinson* (London: Everyman, 1995), p.41.
5 Journal of the House of Commons (HC Journal), (London: HMSO, 1802), II. 29 August 1642, p.743C.
6 Sir C. Firth, and G. Davies, *The Regimental History of Cromwell's Army*, 2 vols (Oxford: OUP, 1940), I, pp. 227–278.

Victorian depiction of Parliamentarian troopers (mounted and unmounted) and foot. (Author's collection)

On the first two occasions, the Nottinghamshire horse charge was broken and Thornhagh, leading the charge, was wounded. At Newark in 1644 his regiment's charge into that of Prince Rupert saw Thornhagh seriously wounded leaving his family and friends despairing for his life. He was carried back to Nottingham in the back of a cart and tended to by both the garrison surgeon and his wife. He did eventually recover, but it took him out of action for around six months. The Nottingham horse enjoyed considerable success at Rowton Heath outside Chester in 1645. Colonel Thornhagh wrote to Parliament after the battle detailing the regiment's actions.

Sir – in pursuit of the King so far I pursued, that retreat I could not, fight I must commending myself and soldiers to God's protection, I resolved to charge them with my regiment. The enemy came on to us, and in a career charged; we stood and moved not till they had fired, which made Gerard swear "God damn him, the rogues will not stir". Upon these words we clapped spurs to our horses, and *gave him such a charge as I dare say was the accomplishment of the victory, for* we routed him and pursued him, which made him fly to Holt castle, over a river in the night, with six men of a thousand, which before were with him.

Francis Thornhagh
September 30[7]

7 British Library (BL), *Perfect Occurrences*, 9 October 1645.

Parliament awarded the Nottinghamshire horse a £1000 reward for their service at Rowton Heath.[8]

Such was the rapport that Thornhagh had with both his offers and troopers that they would follow him into battle even when he asked them to take on different roles to those for which they trained. John Hutchinson recorded one such occasion in January 1644 when Royalist troops under the command of Sir Charles Lucas made a surprise attack on the town of Nottingham and occupied it right up to the walls of the castle. In a subsequent report he acknowledged 'Colonel Thornhagh and all the other horse commanders encouraged their troupers to take muskets to their hands and serve as foot (which to their great glory they very cheerfully and courageously did) and with a foot company joined to part of them, sallied out and beat the cavaliers out of the nearest houses to the castle and possessed them'.[9]

By the end of that day, the forces of Lucas were driven completely out of the town and both the garrison and town were to remain under the control of the Parliamentarians throughout the rest of the first civil war.

Francis Thornhagh's final military experience towards the end of the first civil war was to make him especially useful to Cromwell at Preston. Over the seven-month final siege of Royalist Newark-on-Trent 1645–46, Colonel Thornhagh became increasingly familiar with Scottish military structures and strategies. As one of the senior officers under Poyntz he appears to have been tasked with coordinating joint actions between the English and Scottish armies around the town. The fact that his family estate, at which his mother resided, fell under the jurisdiction of the Scottish forces made him an ideal liaison officer for Poyntz. In this role he became increasingly familiar with command structures within the Scottish army and also the composition, and often lack of discipline, of its field army.

Cromwell and Thornhagh

It is beyond the scope of this chapter to provide in detail the evolving relationship between Thornhagh and Cromwell over the years 1643–1648 but by the time of the Battle of Preston they were well acquainted. We shall therefore just focus on those significant contacts over the period of these five years.

At Whitsun in 1643, following an order issued by parliament the forces of Colonel Cromwell, Colonel Hubbard, Sir John Gell and Lord Grey rendezvous at Nottingham with the forces of Colonel Hutchinson and Colonel Thornhagh. Their instructions were to prevent or hinder the Queen and her newly raised recruits and ammunition train from joining up with the King, then at Oxford. The various Parliamentarian commanders in their many councils and deliberations about how to halt the Queen and her army passing through Nottinghamshire managed to talk themselves into actually doing nothing. According to Lucy Hutchinson, only Cromwell, Hutchinson and Thornhagh argued for taking the field against the Queen's forces, the others demurred. In the end the various Parliamentarian forces drifted away back to their individual garrisons and nothing was done.[10] Cromwell though would have remembered the support of Hutchinson and Thornhagh in seeking military action.

Within weeks, Cromwell and Thornhagh would meet up again on the field of battle outside the Lincolnshire town of Gainsborough on the 28 July 1643. Under the overall command of Sir John Meldrum, the Nottinghamshire and Lincolnshire horse alongside that of Cromwell's went to the relief of the Parliamentarian forces that had recently taken the town but were now besieged by Royalists

---

8 HC Journal, IV, 10 November 1645, p.337.
9 C. H. Firth, *Memoirs of Colonel Hutchinson* (London: Routledge, 1906), Appendix XVIII, p. 418.
10 Keeble, *Lucy Hutchinson*, pp.107–109.

from Newark under the command of Sir Charles Cavendish. The battle was hard fought and involved the Parliamentarian cavalry having to charge the Royalist forces up a steep hill, now known as Foxby Hill. This battle was eventually won by parliament and the Royalists were driven from the field with their commander Charles Cavendish being killed. But having got into the town, it was soon discovered that the whole of the northern Royalist army under the command of the Duke of Newcastle was fast approaching the town. During the strategic withdrawal of the Parliamentarian cavalry, the Nottinghamshire horse was scattered and Thornhagh was captured and subsequently wounded, though he did later manage to escape and re-join Cromwell at Lincoln. One significant outcome of this event was that Thornhagh proved to be amenable to allowing his friend and major Henry Ireton to transfer to Cromwell's regiment and serve under him. Thornhagh needed time to rebuild his shattered regiment and it is most likely that Ireton wanted to see further action sooner rather than later. Whatever the reason, Cromwell and Ireton were not to forget the generosity of Thornhagh's actions.[11]

There survives no evidence of Thornhagh and Cromwell meeting again through the rest of the first civil war. This was because after 1644, Cromwell's regiment was absorbed into the New Model Army whilst Thornhagh and the Nottinghamshire horse were allocated to the Northern Association under the command of Colonel General Sydenham Poyntz in 1645. This doesn't mean that Cromwell lost contact with Thornhagh's military career though. The proximity of the Midlands to the Eastern Association and the fact that Ireton still had relatives living in Nottinghamshire probably meant that information continued to seep through to Cromwell. It was after the election of Thornhagh as an MP for the town of Retford in 1646 that the two men came into each other's orbit again, though now in the House of Commons. Now that the fighting was ending, parliament became increasingly divided over the vexed issues of negotiating a peace with the King and establishing a religious settlement in place of episcopacy. Both these issues had considerable relevance for soldiers who had fought for the cause of Parliament and were owed large arrears of back pay and had enjoyed a degree of religious freedom within their regiments. Thornhagh became

Oliver Cromwell. Print from P. F. Tytler History of Scotland, (Edinburgh: William MacKenzie, 1880). Author's collection.

11   Jennings, *A Very Gallant Gentleman*, pp.42–46.

increasingly identified both as an Independent and, as a commander of a still active horse regiment, a supporter of the army cause over 1647. He served on committees preparing the questions for the Assizes judges and was then appointed soon after to another committee formed to prepare a declaration 'to prevent the Resort and Tumultuous Addresses of all Disbanded Soldiers to the Parliament'. A month later the Colonel was appointed to another committee that was created to facilitate and execute the parliamentary ordinance 'for the sale of the Bishop's Lands'. Fellow Independent politicians hoped that by appointing a serving army officer whom they identified as being sympathetic to a degree of religious freedom to these committees some of the growing angst about the cost of maintaining a standing army might be defused.[12]

Fearing for their safety from the growing tumultuous crowds that were regularly assembling outside Westminster and often encouraged by Presbyterian MPs; 57 independent members, eight peers and the two speakers from both Houses of Parliament fled from Westminster and placed themselves under the protection of Lord Fairfax and the New Model Army. Amongst these politicians were both Francis Thornhagh and John Hutchinson. The political Presbyterians in the Commons, sharing the crowd's animosity towards the expense of maintaining the army and fears of growing religious diversity within its ranks, were not inclined to discourage the crowds. The politics were complex and beyond the brief of this chapter to explore, but Cromwell found in Thornhagh over this period a like-minded individual whom he increasingly warmed to. When the army restored these members back to the Commons, and removed those it had identified as troublemakers, Thornhagh was appointed to serve on further committees.[13] The first he was appointed to sought to consider 'the Payment of the Twenty-eight Thousand pounds to divers reduced and reformed officers' that had served Parliament. He would also serve on two important committees, one to 'prepare proposals outline in Parliament' to put to the King for a peace resolution and the second to prepare an 'Exemption of such tender consciences as cannot conformed to that [Presbyterian] government' of the church.[14] His work on these issues further confirmed his status both to Cromwell and ordinary soldiers as a friend of the army cause. When revolt broke out across England and Wales later in 1648, Cromwell was not averse to having Thornhagh and the Nottinghamshire Horse join him in the campaign in Wales to deal with the rebels there. Thornhagh and his regiment were to serve under Cromwell for the next five months, or in Thornhagh's case until his death on 18 August 1648.

The Road to Preston

On 30 April 1648, Cromwell was ordered to take a detachment of the New Model Army to put down the rebellion underway in south Wales. Those troops of the Nottinghamshire horse still based across in the Midlands, rendezvoused with Cromwell at Gloucester on 8 May. It appears most probable that Thornhagh, already in London working as an MP travelled with Cromwell to Gloucester. At least three troops of Thornhagh's Nottinghamshire regiment had been active on the English and Welsh border long before Cromwell arrived and they too were incorporated into Cromwell's army. Two documents produced in late spring of 1648 had noted their presence under the command of Thornhagh's major Thomas Sanderson. In a letter dated 3 May, it was noted that 'in Herefordshire Major Saunders

---

12   See Jennings, '*A very Gallant Gentleman*', pp.82–87.
13   Journal of the House of Lords, hereafter HL Journal (London: HMSO, 1767–1830), 9, 13 August 1647, pp.385–6.
14   HC Journal, V, 6 October 1647, p.327.

hath quelled the malignants there and taken Col. Sherington prisoner'. On the 6 May, Colonel Thomas Horton reported to Parliament that 'Capt. Creed with three troops of Col. Thornhaugh's regiment doth very good service … being now quartered about Glasbury bridge, which is a good pass near the conjunction of the counties of Hereford, Radnor and Brecon'.[15]

Travelling via Chepstow, Cardiff and Swansea, Cromwell arrived before Pembroke Castle, with Thornhagh and part of his regiment, on the 24 May and began a siege against the well-fortified castle. During such a projected long siege, there was little use for a large force of cavalry by the besiegers and so on the 19 May, Thomas Fairfax reported to Parliament 'I hear that Lieutenant General Cromwell out of his own regiment and Colonel Thornhagh's, hath sent Five Troops of Horse, together with some Dragoons to the confines of Shropshire, Cheshire and North Wales, to whom I shall now send orders to join with Colonel Harrison against the enemy in Lancashire'.[16]

It appears most likely, given Thornhagh's enthusiasm for military action and growing attachment to Cromwell that he stayed with the remainder of his regiment until the end of the siege.

Colonel Francis Thornhagh's regiment was not to be reunited again as a single force until 12 August when Cromwell and Lambert's forces came together at Wetherby to confront the approaching Scottish army. That the Nottinghamshire Horse could be divided up as it was in May, strongly suggests that it was probably nearing full strength, possibly between 500–600 strong. By 1648 the Nottinghamshire Horse no longer consisted of just local troopers, but had recruited from far and wide to make up its numbers. To reach Wetherby, Cromwell brought his army through the Midlands so as to re-equip his soldiers with shoes and shirts. They reached Nottingham at the start of August and spent four days there. The emotional farewell between John Hutchinson and Thornhagh, recorded by Lucy Hutchinson, on leaving to confront the Scots probably reflected the fact that they had been separated for some time, possibly with Thornhagh having been in Wales. For Lucy this was a lasting testimony to the depth of their friendship.

> And at his [Thornhagh's] parting with Colonel Hutchinson took such a kind leave of him, with dear expressions of love and such brotherly embraces and such regrets for any harsh jealousies he had been wrought into, that it took a great impression in the Colonel's kind heart, and might have been a presage to him that thy should meet no more, when they parted with such extraordinary melting, but that Colonel Hutchinson's cheerful and constant spirit never anticipated and evil with fear.[17]

Thornhagh at the Battle of Preston

After Cromwell's rendezvous with Lambert at Wetherby on the 12 August, their combined forces amounted to just over 9,000 men. They then set off across the Pennines to intercept Hamilton's Scottish army, which by then had been supplemented by English Royalists under the command of Marmaduke Langdale. Two days later, Hamilton's army after a council of war set out from Hornby towards Preston, having decided to advance south through Lancashire. This was contrary to the preference of some of his officers who would had preferred a south-easterly march through Yorkshire, as its countryside would offer better conditions for their cavalry to operate in.[18] The poorly trained Scottish infantry, soaked and

---

15 Jennings, 'A Very Gallant Gentleman', p.90–91.
16 HL Journal Journal, 10, 19 May 1648, p.267.
17 Keeble, *Lucy Hutchinson*, p.223
18 Austin Woolrych, *Battles of the English Civil War* (London: Phoenix Press, 1991), pp.164–165.

half-starved, looted mercilessly on their journey south thus alienating any potential support they may have received from Lancashire residents who hitherto were not unsympathetic to the King's cause. The atrocious weather at this time caused further problems for Hamilton's army with the cavalry forced to advance ahead of the infantry in order to find fodder for their horses. By the time the bulk of the Scottish forces had reached Preston on the 16 August, most of their cavalry, under the command of John Middleton, had advanced a further 16 miles southwards towards Wigan seeking fodder for their mounts. Thus Hamilton's forces had become widely dispersed as Cromwell's army advanced towards them.

From Skipton, unsure exactly where the Scottish army was, Cromwell executed a risky plan of launching out towards Preston either to intercept the southwards movement of the Scots or to fall upon their flanks if they had advanced further south. Whilst detachments of Langdale's Royalist Horse had encountered Parliamentarian cavalry around Skipton, the Scots remained unsure exactly where the bulk of Cromwell's army actually was. Three miles west of Clitheroe, Cromwell held a council of war at which the decision was made to keep to the north bank of the river Ribble so as to cut off a potential escape route back to Scotland for Hamilton's forces.

By the late afternoon of the 16 August, Langdale became increasingly aware of a growing number of Parliamentarian cavalry units to the east of Preston. He reported his intelligence to Hamilton, but the Earl of Callander persuaded the duke that if it was anything it was just a vanguard of Cromwell's army. A plan was therefore made to get the bulk of the Scottish infantry across the river and secure

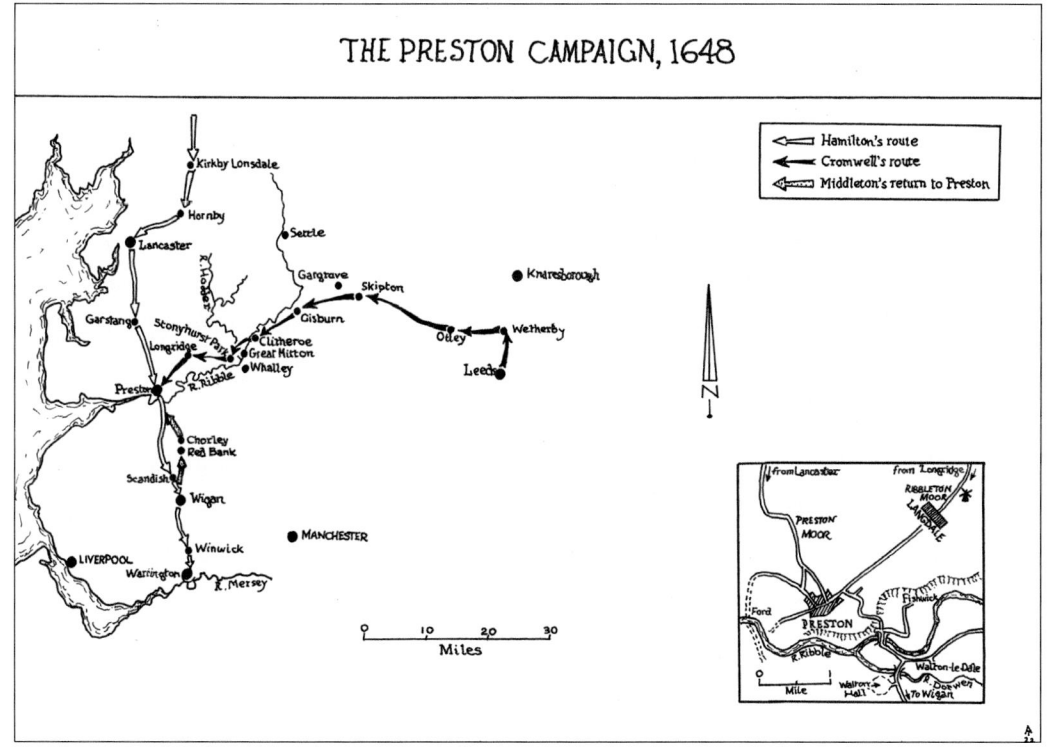

Map of the Preston Campaign, 1648.

the bridges whilst Langdale's Royalist force were to delay the advancing vanguard before withdrawing after the infantry across the river, with cover being provided by the Scottish foot on the opposite bank of the river.

Langdale was furious with Callander's intervention, the former's military experience suggested that this was more than just the approach of a vanguard and he was to be proven correct on the next day. As it was, Langdale positioned his limited Royalist force, consisting of 3,000 foot and 500 horse, on the road into Preston on Ribbleton Moor. This was a deep sunken lane, clogged with mud and bordered by enclosed fields with ditches and hedges, an ideal landscape for musketeers to defend. The fields were waterlogged after all the rain making normal cavalry manoeuvres extremely difficult. This proved to be beneficial to Langdale, for Cromwell's cavalry heavily outnumbered his Northern Horse. Langdale's careful deployment of his forces and the resolve and courage of his soldiers were to hold up the Parliamentarian forces for several hours.[19]

Just before dawn on 17 August, Cromwell's forlorn hope appeared before Langdale's forces. This consisted of 200 horse under the command of Major Smithson and 400 infantry under Major Powell and Captain Hodgson. This force, though experiencing an initial setback when Scottish lancers sent by Hamilton initially engaged with them, kept Langdale's forces engaged until the appearance of Cromwell's main body in the late afternoon. Conditions meant that what followed was no set piece battle but rather bloody hand to hand fighting through the sunken lane all the way back to Preston. This was a task more suited to foot rather than cavalry. The heaviest fighting was in the centre with the regiments of Cromwell, Bright and Reade making little headway until Colonel Ashton's Lancashire foot joined them. At the start of the battle Cromwell had dispatched the cavalry regiments of Thornhagh and Twistleton on his right wing with instructions to try and make their way round to the rear of Langdale. Twistleton's regiment had formerly been the Lincolnshire Horse prior to its absorption into the New Model Army, but its former colonel, Edward Rossiter had been stripped of command. Even so, the two regiments had long served together between 1643–1645 and were used to serving alongside each other. It proved to be a sound manoeuvre by General Cromwell. On the right wing they encountered a body of Hamilton's rear guard cavalry sent to assist Langdale. Both Parliamentarian cavalry regiments performed extremely well and were successful in driving the enemy off the field of battle.

Langdale's forces resisted for up to four hours, according to Cromwell, but finally they broke in the face of overwhelming numbers and large numbers of them were killed or captured in their flight towards Preston. They were especially prone to Cromwell's cavalry in the open fields beyond the lane and the fighting and killing continued right into the centre of Preston itself. By the time that Cromwell's forces had secured Preston and the north bank of the river, after ferocious hand to hand combat, it was getting dark and so a decision was taken to camp out in the fields overnight and rest ready to continue the battle with Hamilton's foot next morning. By the end of the day, the Parliamentarians had captured around 4,000 of Hamilton's men and approximately 1,000 of them had been killed. Though the bulk of Hamilton's army though was still intact, they were demoralised after watching the destruction of Langdale's forces from the opposite bank of the river.[20]

The second stage of the battle began overnight of the 17–18 August. Hamilton called a council of war with his senior officers at which it was decided to attempt the difficult task of silently moving the Scottish army away from the battlefield towards Wigan in order to rendezvous with their cavalry, which

---

19   Malcolm Wanklyn, *Decisive Battles of the English Civil War* (Barnsley: Pen and Sword, 2017), pp.195–196.
20   Peter Young and Richard Holmes, *The English Civil War. A Military History of the Three Civil Wars, 1642–1651* (London: Eyre Methuen, 1974), pp.286–287.

had been summoned back from Wigan. To do this in such a way as not to alert Cromwell's forces to their movement, it was decided to leave all their wagons behind, as the noise of their movement would give them away. The munitions wagons were supposed to be blown up once the army had made its getaway, but this somehow this got overlooked in the retreat and they subsequently fell into the hands of Cromwell's forces next morning. The consequence of this retreat was that the Scottish infantry only possessed the munitions that they could carry with them. This difficult manoeuvre turned into a fiasco when the Scottish cavalry under Middleton coming back from Wigan to assist Hamilton, passed the Scottish infantry in the dark without seeing them. Only when Middleton ran into Cromwell's forward guard at the river Ribble did they realise what had happened.[21]

This action alerted Cromwell to what was occurring and at first light he made arrangements to pursue the Scots. Summoning Francis Thornhagh, he issued a battlefield promotion instructing him and his Regiment of Horse alongside two other regiments placed under his overall command to follow the Scottish forces harrying and delaying them as much as possible whilst Cromwell followed with the rest of his army. For 11 miles Thornhagh successfully followed his orders. Despite courageous cavalry rearguard action by Middleton, the Scots at several skirmishes were driven from the field of battle. The size and quality of the horses in the Parliamentarian cavalry, plus their trooper's extensive military experience, proved critical in these clashes. It was later recorded that Cromwell's soldiers could follow a trail of Scottish corpses by the side of the track all the way to Wigan. Many of these were probably stragglers from the Scottish foot caught up by Thornhagh's cavalry. At one of the skirmishes along the Standish Road, just outside Chorley at a place called Red Bank, Middleton's forces experienced a minor success. Thornhagh, leading a Swedish style charge of the Parliamentarian cavalry, and according to Lucy Hutchinson without full armour, was isolated from his troopers by a group of Scottish lancers and was wounded in his body, thigh and head. He was carried, mortally wounded to the rear of the battle by his own soldiers and lived long enough to witness the triumph of his cavalry over the Scots. Lucy Hutchinson recorded Thornhagh's dying words thus 'I now rejoice to die, since God hath let me see the overthrow of this perfidious enemy; I could not lose my life in a better cause, and I have favour from the Lord to see my blood avenged'.[22]

In the absence of detail about who the other regiments and their officers were, it is now difficult to ascertain who took overall command of the Parliamentarian horse after Thornhagh's death, though it is clear that his major Thomas Saunders took command of the Nottinghamshire horse. They continued to pursue the Scottish horse all the way to Uttoxeter where the latter finally surrendered.

Lucy Hutchinson wrote of Thornhagh's death in her *Memoirs*, that he was 'by mercy removed, that the temptations of the future ties might not prevail to corrupt his pure soul. A man of greater courage and integrity fought not, not fell not, in this glorious cause'.[23]

In this passage she astutely saw both the potential and pitfalls that may have lain in store for Thornhagh had he survived the battle of Preston. In the summer of 1644, Thornhagh had received from parliament a commission to be 'next under Sir Thomas Fairfax, Commander-in-chief of all the Parliament's horse in Nottinghamshire at all times'.[24] At Preston, he had been temporarily appointed to take charge of three regiments of horse to pursue the Scottish infantry, harrying them so as to slow them down. By 1648 then, Thornhagh was one of the senior colonels serving under Cromwell. It seems

---

21 Wanklyn, *Decisive Battles*, pp.190–199.
22 Keeble, *Lucy Hutchinson*, p.225.
23 Keeble, *Lucy Hutchinson*, p.225.
24 Keeble, *Lucy Hutchinson*, p.174.

most likely therefore that he would have received a higher commission after the battle, possibly that of colonel general. This was a rank used by both Royalist and Parliamentarian armies over the English civil war and was a formal designation of a senior colonel. Given that the Nottinghamshire Horse were incorporated into the New Model Army after the ending of the Northern Association early in 1649 and its list of achievements up until its disbandment in 1660, Thornhagh may have even reached the rank of lieutenant general of horse.[25]

Whilst there would have been potential for Thornhagh after Preston, there were also a number of dangers that Lucy foresaw with hindsight that could have led to disaster for the Thornhagh family. Francis Thornhagh had close friendships with a number of the regicides of Charles I and as a sitting independent MP may well have been involved in the trial of the King. His lifelong friend John Hutchinson found himself in this situation, much to the despair of his wife Lucy at the restoration in 1660. As it was, Thornhagh had been dead for six months when Charles was executed and his heir was only around a year old in 1649. Thus, the Thornhagh family suffered no recriminations after the Restoration in 1660. The Nottinghamshire antiquarian Dr Robert Thoroton, a strong Royalist sympathiser with little sympathy for those who had sided with Parliament, felt moved to write of him in 1677 'He was a valiant man, and a colonel of horse for the Parliament, in whose service he lost his life by a scotch lance, as it was said at the battle begun near Preston in Lancashire, between duke Hamilton and that part'.[26]

---

25 I am greatly indebted to Professor Martyn Bennett of Nottingham Trent University for our shared conversations about Thornhagh's potential within the army had he survived Preston.
26 J. Throsby, (ed.), *Thoroton's History of Nottinghamshire*, 3 vols. (Nottingham: J. Throsby, 1790), III, p.296.

A Tale of Two Risings

Peter Gaunt

Was the Second Civil War in England and Wales primarily pro-Royalist or anti-Parliamentarian?

> Our Fathers, which thinke your Howses of Parliament to bee Heaven, you would be honour'd as gods because Charles his kingdome is come unto you; your wills must be donne on earth, as unto the God of Heaven; you have gotten the day, and dispose of our dayly bread; you will not forgive any, neither must you looke to be forgiven; you lead us into rebellion and all other mischeifs, but cannot deliver us from evil. Yours is the kingdome, the power and the glorie, Parliament everlasting, Amen.[1]

This parody of the Lord's Prayer, surviving amongst the papers of a Staffordshire gentleman, is undated, but seems to have been written at some point during the latter half of the 1640s. It reveals a bitter and profound disillusionment with the Long Parliament and its running of affairs in the wake of the full and unconditional victory it had secured in the main civil war of 1642–46. It is just one of many extant writings of the later 1640s to display such sentiments. For example, an equally colourful but much longer text attacking parliament's rule, this time appearing as a printed pamphlet of the opening days of 1648, spoke of how 'The most part of the Kingdom hath been deluded with vain pretences of truth in Religion, of liberty and property, of all earthly happinesse that might be; they expected England to have become a second Paradise. But the Proverb of old, is now to our sorrow found too true, the remedy of these pretenders to Reformation is worse then the disease'. Warming to his theme, the anonymous author went on to expound upon how 'the two Houses have sate above seven yeers to hatch Cocatrices [serpents with power to kill by their glance] and Vipers, they have filled the Kingdom with Serpents, bloodthirstie Souldiers, extorting Committees, Sequestrators, Excisemen, all the Rogues and scumme of the Kingdom have they set on work to torment and vex the people, to rob them, and to eat the bread out of their mouthes …' and so on at length, piling accusation on accusation in portraying parliament's brazen deceit, its betrayal of secular and religious pledges and its wilful establishment of arbitrary government.[2]

---

1   Among the papers of the Royalist Richard Persehouse, at Staffordshire Record Office, D260/M/F/1/6, ff.18–19, transcribed by D.A. Johnson and D.G. Vaisey, *Staffordshire and the Great Rebellion* (Stafford: Stafford County Council, 1964), p.52.
2   *The Declaration of Many Thousands of the City of Canterbury, or County of Kent*, pp.3–4. It carries the printed Old Style date 1647, but was acquired by the bookseller George Thomason on 5 January 1648.

There is abundant and compelling evidence that by the late 1640s many people in England and Wales who had sympathised with and who had actively supported parliament and its cause during the main civil war had become profoundly disillusioned with the course of events since victory had been achieved in early summer 1646 and with the failure of parliament since then either to secure just reforms and a solid and lasting peace or to do away with the novel and unwelcome innovations of the war years, including the unprecedented levels of direct taxation, the new excise duties, the presence of garrisons and the power of their governors, the authority of county committees stuffed with new men and backed by military might and religious uncertainty and disorganisation. By 1647–48 many former Parliamentarians were coming to believe that, through sins of omission and commission, the Long Parliament not only had failed to bring about peace and a return to peace-time conditions but was also deliberately maintaining or intensifying war-time burdens and oppressions. Rather than getting better, things were getting worse.

Equally, however, there were plenty of old Royalists in England and Wales in the later 1640s who did not see 1646 as the end of their hopes or their cause and who were only too willing to resume the fighting in pursuit of a better military outcome. Overt and long-standing royalism also undoubtedly fed into and fuelled many of the disturbances of the late 1640s. Indeed, having expounded upon the dashing of parliamentarian hopes and the betrayal of reformist aspirations by the Long Parliament, the anonymous author of the pamphlet of January 1648 already quoted went on to give vent to some explicitly pro-Royalist sentiments in condemning the members of parliament for their 'causelesse and unnaturall Warre against their own Soveraigne Lord and King, a most pious Christian Prince, contrary to their Allegiance and duty … There is now little mention of the King in any of their proceedings; they voted Him long since not to be in a condition to govern; it is conjectured by us plain Countreymen, that they esteem him but as a conquered Prince, subject now to their mercy; if he could escape with life it were well'.[3]

Accordingly, two strands, anti-Parliamentarianism on the one hand and old Royalism on the other, stoked the riots, risings and renewed fighting seen in many parts of England and Wales during 1648. Some outbursts were distinctly pro-Royalist in origin and character from the very outset, led by those who had openly tied their colours to the king's mast in 1642–46. However, others were more ambiguously anti-Parliamentarian, led by individuals who had previously fought for parliament or breaking out in areas which hitherto had been broadly or even strongly pro-Parliamentarian in outlook and allegiance. Disentangling the two strands as they appear in the surviving contemporary source material is not always easy, not least because, like the Venn diagrams which were such a familiar part of school maths lessons, moderate (politically-Presbyterian) Parliamentarianism and moderate (constitutional) Royalism might overlap.

A flavour of this dichotomy may be found in a clutch of petitions drawn up by or in the name of various counties in the southern half of the country during spring and early summer 1648, just as the second civil war was getting underway.[4] In some cases, these counties were drawn into the renewed civil war and saw military action in the course of the year, though others remained at peace. The latter include Hampshire and Dorset, two counties which had initially come out for parliament in 1642–43,

---

3   *The Declaration of Many Thousands*, p.4.
4   See Robert Ashton, *Counter Revolution; The Second Civil War and its Origins, 1646–48* (New Haven: Yale University Press, 1994), pp.139–53 for a broad review of county petitioning during spring and summer 1648, and John Morrill, *Revolt in the Provinces; The People of England and the Tragedies of War, 1630–1648* (London: Longman, 1999), pp.171–72, 205–6 for briefer but pithy assessments of the petitions and petitioning of that year.

but which had been largely in Royalist hands for much of the main civil war, and in which there was only minor and very limited armed resistance in 1648. The Hampshire declaration was apparently never actually presented to parliament, though it soon appeared as a printed pamphlet, which the London bookseller George Thomason acquired in mid June 1648. It began by noting how some other county petitions had been ignored or rebuffed by parliament. Nonetheless, its authors pulled no punches in deploring the 'almost unsupportable miseries under which this whole Kingdom groanes', drawing particular attention to religion and that 'instead of being reformed, [it] is metamorphis'd into so many shapes', while 'the Synagogue of Rome does exalt'; to 'our heavy Taxes, and other illegall wayes of raising vast Summes, though none of the Royall party have for many months appeared, unless in Prison, or under Sequestration'; to the way that taxes had increased rather than decreased since the end of the war; to how, far from seeking a settlement with him, parliament was keeping the king 'under most barbarous Restraint'; and to how 'our Lawes are fallen into a Lethurgy, [while] Arbitrary power, and the stronger Sword carry all before them'. The authors particularly condemned the failure of parliament to respond to the King's offers to negotiate in pursuit of a settlement, claiming that his approaches were being deliberately blocked by those who wanted to 'square our Religion according to their own confused modules', by those 'that ought to make audit for the many thousands received for the publique … but converted or transported for their own private benefit' and by those who wanted the destruction of monarchical government in order to make 'themselves high and mighty States, and engrossing all Dominion over their yet fellow-Subjects into their own hands'. The solution to all this, the authors concluded, was for the restoration of the Protestant religion as it had been in the days of Elizabeth I and James I, for the return of the King to a 'condition of Safety and Honour' invested with his 'indubitable Rights', for army arrears to be settled and the army quickly disbanded, for accounts to be rendered to show how public money had been spent and for the restored King to pass a broad Act of Oblivion.[5]

The Dorset declaration, which Thomason also acquired in mid June, claimed the support of 10,000 inhabitants of the county. It also opened by noting that the county had 'long groaned under the oppressing tyranny of those whom We deputed for our redeemers' and by highlighting the need to 'wrest Our Soveraign from the jaws of Rebellion and Treason', to vindicate 'our gasping lawes and liberties, from the unrelenting tyranny of those that would bury Both in a Golgotha of their lawlesse wills' and to seek 'the restitution of Protestancy, the reinstatement of his Royall Majesty unto his primitive splendor and greatnesse' and 'an inviolable and well-grounded Peace in all his Majesties Dominions'. There followed a 10 point plan. Some points clearly echoed demands made in the Hampshire petition and in most other county petitions of the time, including the return of the King to London in honour so that he could work directly with parliament, the restoration of the laws to their 'former purity' freed from 'the corrupt Glosses' of 'Arbitrary Power', the reestablishment of the church – in Dorset's case, the petition suggested that an assembly of Protestant divines be set up to advise on this – together with the restoration of the subjects' rights and the rendering of full accounts by all those who had received and spent public money. The Dorset document also called for a new parliament to be elected and for Royalists who had suffered plunder, fines, imprisonment or sequestration to have their property restored and to have the right to seek further redress at law. It was also very critical of the Dorset county committee, giving a social spin to such criticism, as well as of local garrison commanders and their military associates. Thus it requested 'that we may no longer subjugate our necks to the boundlesse

---

5 *The Declaration, Together with the Petition and Remonstrance of the Lords, Knights, Gentlemen, Ministers, and Freeholders of the County of Hampshire* (1648), unpaginated. See also Ashton, *Counter Revolution*, p.148.

lusts, and unlimited power of beggarly and broken Committees, consisting generally of the taile of the gentry, men of ruinous fortunes, and despicable estates, whose insatiate desires, hungry with their frequent wants, prompts them to continuall projects of pilling and stripping us, to repayre themselves'; instead, government was to rest with men of 'visible estates, and unquestioned repute'. Similarly,

> the late imperious Governour of Lyme [Regis] and other of his office, and broken condition, may be no more sheltered under the wings of a membership to glory in the innocent blood of well-meaning Countreymen he hath so unjustly spilt; nor live upon the estates which they have theivishly taken from the right owners, but that they may be exposed to the equall justice of the known Lawes.[6]

Unlike Hampshire and Dorset, Sussex – which had been overwhelmingly Parliamentarian during the main civil war – did experience some violence during summer 1648, though it was very limited and easily quelled. Before this occurred, in early June, a petition was presented to parliament in the name of the people and county of Sussex. It had been drawn up at a meeting held in Lewes in late May and signed copies which survive in the county record office confirm that by 3 June it had attracted around 10,000 signatures, apparently drawn from most of the county and including an array of those who had been active Royalists, active Parliamentarians and more ambiguous neutrals during the first civil war. Much briefer than the two documents already assessed, it noted that in the light of 'the miserable effects' of the civil war, they had five requests to make to parliament, all of them familiar aspirations of counties and county petitions in spring and summer 1648 – that the King be received in safety and honour so that he could work with parliament to secure a firm peace which would safeguard church and state and respect the rights of both crown and parliament; that army arrears be paid and the army then speedily disbanded; that the known laws be followed and respected; that people's estates and goods be freed 'from all Taxes and Impositions'; and that all the county's garrisons be withdrawn, but that the ordnance and ammunition usually held in the Sussex ports be returned so that they could defend themselves and their county from 'foraign Invasions'.[7]

The attempt to present to parliament on 16 May a petition from Surrey – like Sussex, part of the Parliamentarian heartlands during the main civil war – itself provoked an angry and violent confrontation and a little later in the summer the county experienced significant unrest and an attempted Royalist rising. The county's petition which preceded all this was quite brief and although several of its requests were broadly typical of county petitions, the clauses relating to the King were very sympathetic to the royal position and have a Royalist air about them.[8] In order to prevent 'the continuance

---

6   *The Declaration of the County of Dorset* (1648); the quotations are from p.1, 2, 3, 4, 5. Morrill, *Revolt in the Provinces*, pp.171–72, sees the Dorset petition as providing 'the key to the second civil war' in that it was part of a reaction 'against Parliament and centralisation, not *for* the King' (emphasis in the original).
7   *To the Right Honourable the Lords and Commons Assembled in Parliament at Westminster, The Humble Petition of the Knights, Gentry, Clergy and Commonalty of the County of Sussex* (1648), single page broadsheet. See also Ashton, *Counter Revolution*, pp.121–22 for evidence of the gathering of support within Sussex for this petition and p.153 for its contents and reception.
8   A feature also brought out in some of the accounts of the violent confrontations which occurred between members of the Surrey entourage accompanying the petition to Westminster and the soldiers guarding the area, with allegations that some Surrey men cried out 'for God and King Charles' and other Royalist slogans and accused the soldiers of wanting no king in order to justify their attacks upon them. See Ashton, *Counter Revolution*, pp.149–52 and the sources cited there at fn.147. In response, the Surrey men claimed that they were joined in London by a group of Royalists, who latched onto them pretending to be petitioning but who were, in reality, intent on fomenting trouble. *A Declaration of the Knights, Gentlemen, and Freeholders of*

and increase of further evills', the petition urged that the King, 'our only lawfull Soveraign', be restored 'to His due Honour, and just Rights', be returned to his throne in due splendour and be allowed to come to parliament 'with Honour and Safety', in order directly to conclude a treaty with parliament for a firm settlement; that government be by the known laws and statutes; and that parliament prevent 'the unsupportable and most wastfull burthen of Free-quartering of Souldiers' and that, once their arrears had been paid, the army should be disbanded, 'that we may enjoy (without terrours and jealousies) a blessed and long-lookt-for Peace'. Additionally and a little unusually, the Surrey petition also urged parliament to reduce the risk of renewed war 'in this distracted and exhausted Kingdome' by preventing 'by fair Treaty the Forces ready to be brought in from the Neighbour Kingdome' – that is, Scotland and the Scottish-Royalist army then preparing to cross the border – as well from any other nations which might seek to invade.[9]

One of the earliest county petition of this ilk of 1648,[10] drawn up by or in the name of a county which became one of the main centres of the second civil war later in the year, was drafted and agreed at the Essex assize meeting held at Chelmsford on 22 March 1648. Its overall tone, the fact that it was probably the first county petition to call explicitly for parliament to resume negotiations with the King, thereby breaching the vote of no addresses of just a few weeks before, and an accompanying threat of a tax strike in the county until the petitioners' demands had been met, together made it particularly obnoxious to many Parliamentarians and steps were taken to delay and perhaps to attempt to block its presentation. Eventually, it was presented to parliament and read in the House of Commons in mid May, where it was roundly condemned. It opened by noting 'the great distractions and calamities of this whole Kingdom' and the petitioners' 'wofull experience of the great and many pressures and grievances of their own particular County'. In the light of this they had drawn up this 'humble yet necessary addresse'. The petition argued that 'it is impossible the sad and direfull effects of this late War should cease without the principall causes be first taken away and removed' and that the King's absence from parliament was the main impediment to this and the main reason for 'encreasing jealousies, and continuing a misunderstanding' between him and parliament. The petition also drew attention to 'the

---

the County of Surrey (1648), especially pp.4–5. For the Surrey petition and the violence in London associated with its presentation, see also B. Lyndon, 'The South and the start of the second civil war, 1648', *History*, 71 (1986), pp.402–3.

9   *To the Right Honourable Both Houses of the Parliament of England Assembled at Westminster, The Humble Petition of Divers Thousands, nights, Gentlemen, and Freeholders of the County of Surrey, together with the Burrough of Southwark* (1648), single page broadsheet. See also Ashton, *Counter Revolution*, pp.148–53.

10 However, it certainly was not the earliest. For example, a Buckinghamshire petition, drawn up in the wake of parliament's vote of no addresses, was presented to the House of Commons on 9 March. The county had been broadly Parliamentarian during the main civil war, but had suffered Royalist incursions due to the proximity of the King's war-time capital of Oxford, and the petition was very supportive of parliament and thus clearly different from the more ambiguous and sometimes critical tone struck by many of the other county petitions of spring and summer 1648. While it expressed a hope that MPs would continue their 'Honorable endeavors' to settle the government, end free quarter, reduce the size of the army, promote religion and encourage godly ministers, ease the burden of taxation and settle Ireland by crushing 'those Barbarous blood-thirsty Rebels', the petitioners went out of their way to praise parliament's efforts. The text exalted parliament's 'unwearied pains' in pursuing godly and 'faithful endeavours for the good of this Kingdom' and specifically expressed support for the vote of no addresses and terminating negotiations with the King 'after his rejecting so many Applications', as well as lauding the 'ever faithful Army … whom your Petitioners cannot mention without thankfulness'. It was warmly received by MPs and ordered printed. *The Humble Petition and Representation of many Inhabitants of the County of Buckingham* (1648); the quotations are from p.3, 4, 5, 6.

excessive charges and almost intolerable burthen this County, with the rest of the Kingdome, doe at this present groane under' and which if continued would 'certainly and inevitably ruine themselves, their families and posterities', noting too that army pay was in arrears. The solution to all these problems was for direct negotiations to be opened between King and parliament, leading to a settlement. The petition concluded by requesting that parliament would 'condescend to the royall intimations of his Majesty for a Personall Treaty'. In its closing sentence, it also revealed its authors' preferred solution for lowering taxes and removing military discontent, requesting parliament 'to expedite such a course which in your wisdomes you shall think most meet for the satisfaction of the arreares of the Army, with the disbanding of the same'.[11] In Essex – another county which had formed part of the Parliamentarian heartlands throughout the main civil war and which had appeared firmly committed to the Parliamentarian cause in the early and mid 1640s – as in so many other counties, the mood had clearly changed by 1648.

While there were significant overlaps between and common elements found within these and other county petitions of spring and summer 1648, some conclusions can tentatively be drawn. Some petitions seem rooted in Royalism and in established and continuing support for the King, but others showed no real evidence of Royalism in their texts and instead are better characterised as anti-Parliamentarian, springing from disillusionment with and opposition to aspects of parliament's post-war government and administration, both at the centre and in the localities. Some issues highlighted might draw on both elements, particularly the failure of parliament to reach a firm settlement with the King, to the dismay of long-standing Royalists and also of some of those who had hitherto supported the Parliamentarian cause. Equally, some petitions and manifestos may quite consciously and deliberately have been framed in order to win support from both camps. It is quite possible, though it generally cannot be proved, that Royalist authors and participants toned down the pro-Royalist nature of some of their demands and supported wider complaints about the nature of parliament's post-war government in order to broaden the platform and appeal of the resulting petition and thus hope to win support from disillusioned Parliamentarians. It is possible, though perhaps less likely, that the opposite is true of some of the county petitioning programmes of spring and summer 1648.

Different factors and shades of old and new allegiance can also be detected in the different theatres where sporadic, or more organised and widespread, violence broke out during the so-called second civil war in the course of 1648, from Norwich and Bury St Edmunds in East Anglia to Penzance and the Lizard in the far south west, from parts of Surrey and Sussex in the south east to Caernarvonshire and the Isle of Anglesey in north-west Wales, from Shropshire and Herefordshire in the West Midlands across to the area around Stamford and Peterborough in the East Midlands. However, given the limits of space, the rest of this chapter will focus on the two principal home-grown risings of the second civil war – that which began in Kent but which spilled over into Essex and culminated in the long siege of Colchester, and that which began in south Pembrokeshire before quite briefly spreading to other parts of south Wales, notably Glamorganshire, but which culminated in the long siege of Pembroke.

The main rising in Kent, which began with growing disorder in parts of the county in May 1648 and which seemed to be gaining pace until nipped in the bud by Sir Thomas Fairfax and part of the New Model Army, who engaged and defeated a rebel force at Maidstone on 1 June, but which then

---

11 *To the Right Honourable both Houses of the Parliament of England, Assembled at Westminster, The Humble Petition of the Grand Jury at the Assizes Holden at Chelmsford, for the County of Essex* (1648), single page broadsheet. See also Ashton, *Counter Revolution*, pp.142–44 and B. Lyndon, 'Essex and the King's cause in 1648', *Historical Journal*, 29 (1986), pp.21–22.

spilled over into parts of Essex, can most obviously be portrayed as pro-Royalist in nature more or less from the outset.[12] Thus active leadership generally and from its early days rested with figures who had a clear and established pedigree of Royalism. In the course of May George Goring senior, 1st Earl of Norwich (of a new creation), was accepted as General and military leader of the rising, in part on the grounds of his long service to the King and established Royalist credentials, even though he was by then in his sixties, had limited prior military experience and had spent much of the main civil war abroad.[13] Once the surviving Kentish rebels had crossed into Essex, they were joined by other prominent and long-standing Royalists, including for a time by Lords Capel and Loughborough, as well as by Sir Charles Lucas and Sir George Lisle during the Colchester phase. Not only was the leadership distinctly Royalist throughout, but also several of the key declarations and manifestoes which the rebel movement drew up and issued had a broadly or explicitly pro-Royalist tone. This is apparent in the document which in many ways was the catalyst for the Kentish rising, a petition drawn up by or in the name of the people of Kent and dated 11 May. The text, drafted at an informal meeting of the Kentish grand jury in Canterbury, was fairly brief and crisp and, after noting the 'miseries' and 'sufferings' of Kent and other counties, it made four specific requests of parliament. The first and chief of these was that the King 'be admitted in safety and Honour, to Treat in person with his two Houses of Parliament for the perfect setling of the Peace both of Church and Common Wealth, as also of his owne just rights, together with those of Parliament'.[14]

The broadly Royalist tone of this first demand, together with a call speedily to disband the Parliamentarian army, ensured that the petition met with a hostile response both from parliament and from parliament's county boss in Kent, Sir Anthony Weldon, who sought to deploy troops to prevent the circulation of the petition within the county. In practice, the attempt failed and may have served only to encourage wider support for the petition, which by late May had supposedly gained 20,000 signatures within Kent. But the Royalist leadership of the growing Kentish rising must have been aware that the county had been predominantly, if sometimes a little uneasily, Parliamentarian throughout the main civil war. Accordingly, even though Norwich and his old Royalist allies were probably behind them, both a *Manifest* (or Manifesto) and *A Remonstrance* issued later in May said nothing about acting for the King. Instead, the texts of both these key documents sought to portray the rising as a move to defend the legitimate rights of the county and its people in the face of stern threats being posed by the

---

12 The most detailed modern account of the Kentish rising is A. Everitt, *The Community of Kent and the Great Rebellion, 1640–60* (Leicester: Leicester University Press, 1973), chapter 7. The events generated a lot of contemporary printed material, including pamphlets and reports in the London newspapers; particularly interesting, despite its clearly partisan nature, is the unusually detailed account of events in Matthew Carter, *A Most True and Exact Relation of that as Honourable as Unfortunate Expedition of Kent, Essex and Colchester* (1650), written from the perspective of a participant in the rebellion – he became Norwich's quartermaster – and in some ways balancing the pro-Parliamentarian line taken by most of the contemporary printed material.

13 B. Donagan, 'George Goring, First Earl of Norwich (1585–1663)', *Oxford Dictionary of National Biography*, online edition at https://doi.org/10.1093/ref:odnb/11101 [accessed 1 January 2023]. Donagan comments that it is not clear whether Goring had been specifically sent to Kent to take charge of the rising or whether it was just good fortune that he was on the spot, on route to his main property in neighbouring Sussex. Either way, she speculates that it was his conciliatory skills and his familiarity within the county through family connections that led to his acceptance and appointment 'as general of the royalist forces' of Kent in late May.

14 *To the Right Honourable the Lords and Commons Assembled in Parliament at Westminster, The Humble Petition of the Knights, Gentry, Clergy, and Commonalty of the County of Kent* (1648); the quotations are from p.2. See also Ashton, *Counter Revolution*, pp.144–48.

Long Parliament, by its Kentish county committee, which was attempting 'to involve this County in bloud', and by Weldon, who had allegedly 'vowed he would not crosse the Street ... to save one soul that subscribed to the Petition' of 11 May and who was being urged by one of his cronies 'to hang two of the Petitioners in every Parish'.[15]

These threats played into the hands of the Royalist leadership in their rebranding of the movement as a much broader and less partisan defence of local and Kentish rights. Thus the *Manifest* stressed, not their support for the king, but the 'innocency of our intentions, and justice of all our undertakings', claiming that

> our assembling and meeting together ... is no other then for a vindication of ourselves ... from the scandall, and aspersions of the Committee of this County; who upon occasion of a Petition in behalf of the County of Kent ... have not onely made Orders against the same ... condemning the said Petition and all the Abettors thereof ... [but] have summoned the Troups of Horse, and Forces of Foot ... for suppression of the said Petition; which tends not only to the suppression of ... Liberty ... but also ... an endeavour ... to over-awe the senses of other men, and upon opposition ... think they have ground enough to take away the lives and fortunes, or both, of their said opposers.

Accordingly, the committee, by attempting 'to involve the County in bloud' and maliciously misrepresent the petition and petitioners to parliament, was forcing Kent to respond and to put itself 'in a posture of Defence', viewing 'all opposition, as the provocation of a conscious and enraged Committee' and, rather than being 'at the mercy of Souldiers, ... to have refuge to our Armes, from which no threats, or face of Souldiery shall drive us'.[16] Again, while Royalist activists in Kent were probably involved in preparing the county's *Remonstrance*, it claimed that the people of Kent were being forced either 'to deliver up our Lives and Liberties together, or to dye free', compelled 'to act the last Scene of this Tragedy with our Swords in our hands' in response to the direct threats of Weldon and his allies. Those who accepted and signed the document were to engage

> solemnly and Religiously [to] oblige ourselves, with our Lives and Fortunes, to oppose effectually, what Person or Persons soever shall presume to interrupt us in the just and Legall presentment of our humble desires to the two Houses of Parliament; and to the utmost of our endeavours to save harmelesse and protect each other ... And further, in Case any single person shall be for this Engagement prosecuted, All of us to rise as one Man to the rescue.[17]

In both these key documents, therefore, the Kentish rising was being recast as the (only) means by which the county and its people could protect themselves from unwarranted violence and shocking violation; the King himself and the Royalist cause more broadly had disappeared from view.[18]

---

15 *The Manifest of the County of Kent* (1640), single page broadsheet; *A Remonstrance Shewing the Occasion of the Arming of the County of Kent* (1648), single page broadsheet.
16 *Manifest of the County of Kent*, single page broadsheet.
17 *Remonstrance Shewing the Occasion of the Arming of the County of Kent*, single page broadsheet.
18 The same is true of another document which circulated in Kent at this time and which claimed to have garnered the support of 27,000 inhabitants; quite brief and not especially outspoken, it stressed that the county was being threatened and that its people would not stand idly by while their 'religion, Lawes, lives and fortunes' were sacrificed. *A Declaration of the Counties of Kent and Essex* [a pamphlet reproducing the texts of two separate county documents] (1648), unpaginated.

Thus while active leadership of the increasingly war-like Kentish movement generally rested with figures who had clear Royalist sympathies or backgrounds, some of them natives of the county with a Royalist pedigree, others outsiders who travelled to Kent to strengthen what was rapidly turning into one of the most promising areas for the King's cause, the more perceptive Royalists probably realised that if they were to attract and to retain widespread support in a county with a strong Parliamentarian record, they would need to be careful not to overplay support for the King and instead to stress that they were promoting a defensive movement aimed at securing both the county's rights and liberties and a wider settlement. This approach worked quite well and, despite some signs of divisions between committed Royalists and moderates, as well as initially fruitless attempts by parliament to widen them by seeking to open discussions with the moderates, the Kentish movement held together long enough to mount armed resistance to Sir Thomas Fairfax and his New Model Army regiments. However, the rising in Kent was effectively broken in a single battle, at Maidstone, scuppered certainly by parliament's decisive military response and by the greatly superior military force which Fairfax deployed in the county. But perhaps it was also weakened by lurking tensions and divisions between an explicitly Royalist core and leadership on the one hand and large numbers of fellow-travellers on the other, petitioners and supporters of petitions who were disillusioned with parliament and with parliament's response in the spring and who for a time made common cause with the Royalists, drawn in by their carefully-worded public documents, but whose commitment to armed rebellion against parliament faltered when faced with cold realities and the New Model Army.[19]

Moreover, if we are fully to understand the nature of the Kentish rising of spring 1648, we need to take account of its antecedents. While the immediate catalyst of the Kentish rising was the petition of 11 May, sympathetic to the King's position, drawn up by or in the name of the people of Kent at a gathering of the county's grand jury at Canterbury, that in turn was a consequence of earlier events in the town. A riot had taken place at Canterbury at the end of 1647, triggered by the attempts of the Parliamentarian authorities to restrict or prevent Christmas festivities, in accordance with parliamentary ordinances. The mayor – an 'Excise-man and also a man of a rough and unkind nature'[20] – directed that shops remain open and a market be held on Christmas day, but a mob scuppered his orders, forcing their closure and smashing the wares of the few shops which did try to open and then skirmishing with the mayor and sheriff when they attempted to apprehend ringleaders. Far from obeying the mayor's orders to disperse and go home, the crowd produced a couple of footballs and began a street game which soon attracted an even bigger crowd, some of them reportedly drawn into Canterbury from the surrounding countryside, and a general 'tumult' ensued. Parliamentarian civic officials and godly ministers were threatened, attacked or frightened off, holly bushes and other traditional Christmas decorations were put up, alehouses were opened and did a roaring trade and the merry-making but at times rowdy or hostile crowd continued to grow.[21] Disorder escalated over the following days, with further attacks upon the houses and, if they tried to intervene, the persons of civic officials and Parliamentarian committeemen, with occasional shots discharged by pistols or muskets and with the breaking open of the town jail, while the magazine was also ransacked. Smaller but broadly similar copy-cat outbreaks began in a few other Kentish towns.

---

19   That is very much the interpretation followed and conclusion reached by Everitt, *Community of Kent and the Great Rebellion*, chapter 7.
20   *A Letter from a Gentleman in Kent* (1648), pp.2–3.
21   *A Letter from a Gentleman in Kent*, and *Canterbury Christmas, or a True Relation of the Insurrection in Canterbury on Christmas Day Last* (1648).

In fact, things were quickly brought under control when Weldon and some members of parliament's county committee, who were not in Canterbury at the time, called out the county militia and other troops. They swiftly restored order in other towns and isolated and surrounded Canterbury itself, which surrendered without a fight in early January 1648. The town's gates and stretches of its walls were demolished, Parliamentarian troops with artillery pieces were stationed in the town, rebel leaders were arrested and imprisoned and Weldon sought from parliament permission to proceed against them by martial law. In this he was unsuccessful and parliament directed that the prisoners be tried by normal assizes. This failed to defuse the situation, for when the trials eventually got underway in May 1648 and the Kentish grand jury proved recalcitrant and sympathetic to the accused, Parliamentarian attempts to pressurise the jurymen and to secure their prosecution and conviction provided a focus and a rallying point for Kentish discontent. It was this that served as one of the key triggers of the Kentish petition of 11 May and the county's stand during the spring.[22]

In order fully to understand the nature of the Kentish rising of spring 1648 it is therefore necessary to explore the nature of the Canterbury riot of Christmas 1647, as the repercussions of that event led onto and precipitated the May petition, which in turn triggered the wider county rising. Alas, like many short-lived and geographically-limited outbursts of the period, that is hard to do, despite the fairly full coverage of the course of events at Canterbury found within the pamphlets and London-based newspapers of the day. Some declarations issued by or in the name of the Canterbury rioters around this stage, most notably the *Declaration of Many Thousands of the City of Canterbury* which Thomason acquired on 5 January, and which has already been drawn upon and quoted in the introductory section of this chapter, were in some parts distinctly Royalist in tone, expressing strong support for the King and for the restoration of royal powers, while also, perhaps with an eye on winning over moderate Parliamentarians, calling for the preservation of parliament and its just rights and powers.[23] However, other accounts, including some written by participants, strongly denied any Royalist allegiance or intention and claimed merely to be acting in response to non-partisan local grievances triggered by the attitude of the mayor and his officers.[24] Again, some of the earliest third person reports printed in pamphlets and newspapers did not discern any clearly Royalist element to or within the disturbances. For example, the anonymous author of *Canterbury Christmas*, which Thomason also acquired at the beginning of January, portrayed the riot as a genuinely localist response to the heavy-handed approach taken and the violence offered by the mayor, the sheriff and some aldermen.[25] However, other accounts noted that, once the outburst was well underway and outsiders had been drawn into the town as the crowds swelled, '*At last* the Cry was, For God, King Charles, and Kent' (emphasis added), hinting – though certainly not explicitly stating – that the initial Canterbury rising had acquired a noticeably Royalist rallying cry and complexion only once non-townsmen from further afield had joined it.[26]

---

22 The fullest modern account, both of the events in Canterbury at Christmas and their links with the developments and petition of the following May, is in Everitt, *Community of Kent and the Great Rebellion*, pp.231–40.
23 *Declaration of Many Thousands of the City of Canterbury, or County of Kent.*
24 Letter to Sir John Culpeper at Bodleian Library, Clarendon Ms. 31, f.96, cited by Everitt, *Community of Kent and the Great Rebellion*, p.231, fn.2.
25 *Canterbury Christmas, passim.*
26 *A Perfect Diurnall of Some Passages in Parliament*, no. 231, 27 December–3 January 1647[8], p.1861, one of several newspapers which went to press during the first two weeks of January to make this claim and to carry this report.

Norwich and around 3,000 of his Kentish rebels who survived the *debacle* at Maidstone crossed the Thames, entered Essex and eventually occupied and then tried to hold out in Colchester, joined by other prominent Royalists of clear and long-standing pedigree, notably Capel and Loughborough, Lucas and Lisle. Their increasingly desperate and precarious hold on the city through the resulting 11 week Parliamentarian siege mounted by Fairfax is very well documented in contemporary, mainly printed, accounts, and the whole operation has been explored afresh by several recent historians.[27] By and throughout this stage of the rising, from the arrival of Norwich and his Kentish force during the second week of June until the eventual surrender of the closing days of August, the resistance mounted within Colchester, its leadership, rhetoric and overall tone were explicitly and unambiguously pro-Royalist in appearance and come across as driven by strong and genuine Royalism. However, as in the earlier Kentish phase, once again the origins of the events in Essex are more complex and nuanced.

We have already noted that in late March Essex had drawn up a county petition addressed to parliament, calling for King and parliament to resume negotiations towards a national settlement. Printed copies were circulated around the county during April and at a series of meetings and gatherings it gained broad support and many signatures, ahead of its formal presentation to parliament on 4 May. It was not a particularly outspoken petition, the process of holding county meetings and garnering support seems to have been fairly peaceful and orderly, its presentation to both Houses passed off without incident and parliament responded with thanks and a fairly bland promise to take matters into consideration.[28] However, below this reasonably calm and orderly surface, there was an undercurrent of discontent within the county, directed at the continuing high taxes, exacerbated by economic depression and unemployment, at perceived abuses by troops stationed within the county and at the failure of parliament to reach a clear religious settlement. Moreover, during the spring some within Essex were agitating for a much harder and stronger line to be taken in pursuit of county grievances. In mid May there appeared in print a much sharper and more strident series of demands in the form of an 'Ingagement', perhaps modelled on the Kentish engagement, put out in the county's name and supposedly agreed at a county meeting. It called for no further payment of excise until its demands had been met and for no troops to be allowed into the county other than those signifying support for the county's petition and for this engagement; its adherents pledged to 'imploy our utmost endeavers to preserve and defend our Royall Soveraigne King Charles, his Kingly Government, the Subjects liberty, and the known Lawes of the Kingdom' – it said not a word about parliament's rights; and its supporters were to 'protect and defend one another and all that shall adhere to us, in the pursuance, performing, and keeping of this Ingagement', while any in Essex refusing to join them 'we shall esteeme as a person

---

27 Diaries or day-by-day accounts of (parts of) the operation can be found at *An Exact Narrative of Every Days' Proceedings Since the Insurrection in Essex* (1648), *A Diary of the Siege of Colchester by the Forces under the Command of General Fairfax* (1648) and 'The siege of Colchester' in Historical Manuscripts Commission, *Twelfth Report, Appendix Part IX. The Manuscripts of the Duke of Beaufort, K.G., the Earl of Donoughmore, and Others* (London: 1891), pp.19–31. Numerous contemporary accounts of (part or all of) the siege appeared in the newspapers of the day and as separate pamphlets, including most usefully Carter, *Most True and Exact Relation, A Great and Bloody Fight at Colchester* (1648), *Colchester's Tears* (1648), Sir T. Fairfax, *A Letter from his Excellency the Lord Fairfax General of the Parliament's Forces, Concerning the Surrender of Colchester* (1648) and T. S., *A True and Exact Relation of the Taking of Colchester* (1648). For recent assessments, see P. Jones, *The Siege of Colchester, 1648* (Stroud: Tempus, 2003) and B. Donagan, *War in England, 1642–1649* (Oxford: Oxford University Press, 2008), chapters 15–18, incorporating key material from her earlier articles exploring the siege of Colchester.

28 *To the Right Honourable both Houses of the Parliament of England ... The Humble Petition ... for the County of Essex*, which carries the text of the petition as well as giving a brief narrative of key events down to 4 May.

disaffected to the peace, and welfare of the same'. It went on to call for a purge of disloyal officers and men from the county militia, the raising of further troops in Essex by 'such Gentlemen thereof, in whom they may repose trust' and a muster of all the county's troops.[29]

The document and its programme may have sprung from and been written and circulated by a group of disgruntled militia officers, including a Major Smith and Lieutenant Colonel Henry Farr, who had a number of grudges but whose ire seems mainly to have been directed against the Essex county committee. They proceeded to hold a series of musters in late May and early June, increasingly hostile to parliament and parliament's county committee, culminating in a meeting in Chelmsford on 4 June at which they effectively took control of the town and seized several members of the county committee who had been meeting there. Thus the foremost historian of the Essex troubles in 1648, Brian Lyndon, concludes that they sprang from military discontent and mutinies amongst Parliamentarian forces and their officers within the county, in some ways reminiscent of the string of mutinies in parliament's provincial armies during 1646–7, and that their adoption of a semi-Royalist line in some of their documents 'was, therefore, cynical and mercenary'.[30] Lyndon paints a convincing picture of Essex discontent in spring and early summer 1648 as grounded in a range of issues – military discontent amongst some locally-based Parliamentarian units, dislike of parliamentary taxation given extra edge by the county's financial situation and apprehension caused by drift and uncertainty in religion – which were anti-Parliamentarian and not conspicuously pro-Royalist in origins and nature. However, those grievances, the local discontent to which they were giving rise and many of the active protesters already on the streets were then swept up into, subsumed within, perhaps even hijacked by, the Royalist leadership and their bigger and more organised pro-Royalist rising advancing across the county and then making a stand in Colchester.[31] Thus at first glance, both the Kent and Essex phases of the second civil war appear to be Royalist risings, albeit that as they unfolded the Royalist element and rhetoric were deliberately toned down, even disguised, and a pitch made by the leadership to appeal to disgruntled Parliamentarians within two counties which hitherto had been predominantly Parliamentarian in outlook and allegiance. However, closer use of the surviving contemporary evidence suggests that that is too simple an interpretation and that in Kent and Essex alike there is more to the origins and early course of events than might initially meet the eye.

At first glance, too, the opposite might seem true and self-evident of the other major home-grown English and Welsh rising of spring and summer 1648, that which began and ended at Pembroke but which spread more widely across parts of southern Pembrokeshire and for a time into Carmarthenshire and Glamorganshire.[32] Here the rising was intimately linked with the stand taken by a trio of

---

29 *Declaration of the Counties of Kent and Essex* [the texts of two separate county documents], unpaginated.
30 Lyndon, 'Essex and the king's cause in 1648', especially p.25, from which the quotation is taken, Lyndon, 'Parliament's army in Essex, 1648', *Journal of the Society for Army Historical Research*, 58 (1980) and Lyndon, 'The South and the start of the second civil war'.
31 An interpretation offered within or underpinning Lyndon's trio of key articles, but at its clearest in his 'Essex and the King's cause in 1648', which emphasises the increasing Royalist influence and leadership at Chelmsford and of the Colchester phase, pp.26–29, and that while the rank and file may have been more mixed, 'local militancy was superintended by Cavalier officers and mobilised in a cause which was not localist but national and partisan' (that is, pro-Royalist), pp.35–36.
32 The two best modern accounts are R. Matthews, *'A Storme Out of Wales'. The Second Civil War in South Wales, 1648* (Newcastle upon Tyne: Cambridge Scholars Press, 2012) and L. Bowen, *John Poyer. The Civil Wars in Pembrokeshire and the British Revolutions* (Cardiff: University of Wales Press, 2020). As the titles make clear, Matthews examines the whole of the south Wales rising, while Bowen focuses more on Poyer and his actions at Pembroke and in (south) Pembrokeshire.

Parliamentarian officers, John Poyer, Rice Powell and Rowland Laugharne, with Poyer very much the leading light, at least in the early stages. All three had been from the outbreak of the main civil war steadfast supporters of parliament, valiantly resisting the Royalism and royalist forces which dominated almost the whole of Wales, including South Wales, throughout that war. Marooned and outnumbered though they were, they had been brave and resolute in their defence of parliament's south Pembrokeshire enclave, holding out in just about the only part of Wales where genuine and popular Royalism was not the dominant mood, even when they had been pinned back into little more than Pembroke and Milford Haven. Yet in 1648 these parliamentarian heroes of the main civil war, with Poyer to the fore, initiated and led an equally resolute and armed stand against the Long Parliament, the New Model Army high command and Parliamentarian administrators and army units on the ground in south-west Wales, doing so in the very same towns and parts of southern Pembrokeshire which had been parliament's beleaguered but loyal toe-hold in Royalist Wales for most of the war years.

Through the recent work of Lloyd Bowen, we can now be much clearer about what motivated Poyer, in particular, to take this stand during the winter and opening months of 1648. A Pembrokeshire man of quite modest origins and standing, as mayor of Pembroke and governor of the castle and Parliamentarian garrison in the town for most of the main civil war, his resolute support for parliament, combined with a sometimes tactless but forceful manner and administrative approach, had served to retain parliament's hold over Pembroke. But at the same time he had alienated a group of Pembrokeshire gentry, the Lorts and the Eliots prominent among them, who had flowed with the ebb and flow of the tide in Pembrokeshire during the war years and who had sometimes worked with the King's forces when Royalism was in the ascendant in the region. But it was these men who had won the trust and favour of the Long Parliament and the New Model high command in the post-war years and, resentful of Poyer and his clique, they used their positions of local power and influence to attempt to destroy him. When, early in 1648, Fairfax was persuaded to replace him as governor of Pembroke, Poyer faced the prospect of losing his powerbase and having no defence against his local opponents, now in power and running Pembrokeshire for parliament, who were circling, determined not only to deny Poyer's claims for arrears of pay and payment of other expenses incurred during the main civil war, but also to pursue him for alleged financial corruption. For good measure, they were also blackening him for alleged moral and sexual laxity, for fathering several bastards and, perhaps just as damning in their eyes, for beginning life as a mere 'turn-spit boy' working in a kitchen and as 'a poore ragged boy … hired to run to and fro on errands'.[33] Outmanoeuvred and at risk of being left powerless and defenceless, this seems to have been what motivated Poyer and in due course his two colleagues to take a stand and, supported by many of their troops who remained loyal to them, with increasing violence to resist attempts to remove them from Pembroke Castle and their other strongholds, notably Tenby, to strip them of their military commands and to disband their troops.[34]

Bowen's research largely reinforces and convincingly fleshes out that interpretation and confirms that there was nothing directly or even indirectly Royalist or supportive of the King and his cause behind the stand Poyer and others took during the opening weeks of 1648. The various declarations and other statements which they issued in February and March, as their resistance hardened and became more violent, made no reference to favouring or working for the King. Royalists further afield began taking an interest in the activities of Poyer, Powell and Laugharne, hoping that they would come out for the

---

33 *A Declaration of Divers Gentlemen of Wales Concerning Colonell Poyer* (1648); the quotation is from p.2. Poyer vigorously denied the allegations in detail in J. Poyer, *Poyer's Vindication in Answer to a Lying Pamphlet* (1649).
34 Matthews, *'A Storme Out of Wales'*, especially chapter 2; Bowen, *John Poyer*, especially chapters 3–5.

King, but at this stage there is no discernible sign that Poyer and his colleagues were even preparing to do so. Indeed, the very opposite, for several times during February and March Poyer portrayed himself in print as a still loyal supporter of parliament, willing to obey the orders of the Long Parliament and Sir Thomas Fairfax so long as his men were paid and treated well, his own arrears and other expenses were met and he was given an unambiguous indemnity protecting him from future prosecution for alleged financial corruption or any other actions he had taken during the main civil war. For example, in a declaration and set of propositions dated 13 March and in response to a summons to surrender, he indicated that he and his men would disband and peacefully hand over Pembroke Castle if their full arrears were paid, he received a further £1,000 to cover his own war-time expenses and losses and he and his men then had liberty to march away.[35] During February Laugharne and some of his officers also sent a petition to Fairfax in which they offered to disband if they received guarantees that the money owing to them would be paid, and neither delayed nor denied them by the Pembrokeshire committee, and if they also received compensation for the loss of or damage to their estates,[36] while the following month they again stressed their long pedigree of Parliamentarianism and denied disloyalty or rebellion, claiming that their opponents within Pembrokeshire were unjustly slurring them along those lines.[37]

Down to late March, then, there is little indication that Poyer, Powell and Laugharne were acting on behalf of the King or were overt or covert Royalists. They had hitherto been loyal Parliamentarians and, despite their increasingly forceful refusal to obey orders, thus far even most of their opponents do not seem to have seen them as or accused them of supporting the King; 'rebels' rather than royalists was how they were generally labelled in the Parliamentarian press by the latter half of March. An exception, a letter appearing in a London newspaper in mid March, which claimed that Poyer, often drunk, was acting very erratically, at times pretending or perhaps genuinely being in contact with the Prince of Wales and to be supporting his father's cause, is convincingly dismissed by Bowen as a concoction of the Lord-Eliot faction designed to discredit Poyer.[38] But in late March, with loyal Parliamentarian troops threatening Pembroke and New Model reinforcements on their way, Poyer altered his stance.

First, Poyer decided to lead a military strike on the fairly modest Parliamentarian force outside Pembroke, calling on some of Laugharne's men to come to his support, so that their opponents would be caught between the two. According to a report written by a John Wilson in Gloucester a few days later, on 28 March, the Parliamentarians 'defended themselves gallantly, for the space of half an hour' against a frontal attack from Poyer, but they were 'over-powred' when reinforcements arrived and were compelled to fall back, losing several dead and 'many … wounded', while between 20 and 30 were captured and carried prisoner into Pembroke Castle, as were arms and ammunition and two large artillery pieces which had been deployed against the castle.[39] Probably aware that he had initiated a clear act of war, Poyer strengthened his hold over the town and castle of Pembroke, raising further money,

---

35   J. Poyer, *The Declaration and Resolution of Col. John Poyer* (1648), pp.4–5.
36   'The Humble Petition of the Officers under the command of Major Generall Laughorne', undated but reportedly received by Fairfax on 25 February, is printed in *A Perfect Diurnal of Some Passages in Parliament*, no. 239, 21–28 February 1648, pp.1926–27.
37   The petition of the officers to the House of Commons, undated but received by the House in early March, is printed in *The Kingdom's Weekly Post*, no. 9, 2–9 March 1648, pp.68–69; 'A declaration in Vindication of the Officers and Souldiers under the command of Major Generall Laughorne, from divers false reports, and slanderous assertions cast upon them', agreed at Carmarthen on 10 March, is printed in *A Bloody Slaughter at Pembrooke Castle in Wales* (1648), pp.4–6.
38   *A Perfect Diurnall of Some Passages in Parliament*, no. 243, 20–27 March 1648, p.1955; Bowen, *John Poyer*, pp.122–23.
39   Poyer, *Declaration and Resolution*, pp.2–3.

supplies and troops in early April and also successfully capturing or repulsing the first significant batch of Parliamentarian reinforcements arriving in the area, who had travelled by boat from Bristol and landed on the south shore of Milford Haven.

Second, Poyer and his allies shifted their position in a crucial way. Until early April, there is little indication that Poyer, Laugharne and the other protagonists who were opposing disbanding and disobeying orders were acting for the King or supporting his cause. The report of Poyer's much more aggressive military action written by Wilson in Gloucester at the end of March included, tucked away amidst news of what Laugharne and his men were up to in and around Tenby, a comment that 'Here is great talk in these parts, of the raising of a new Army for the King, the Royal party giving out very high speeches'; in the context, it seems more likely that Wilson's 'in these parts' was referring to southern Pembrokeshire or perhaps more broadly south Wales than to the Gloucester area where he was then writing, but even if that was the case, Wilson was not directly or explicitly claiming that Laugharne and his men were themselves talking about raising or acting to raise new forces for the King.[40] Thus far Poyer and his key allies in southern Pembrokeshire appear to have been fomenting and leading an increasingly strident mutiny against Parliamentarian orders, prompted by the planned disbandment and its consequences, led by a group of Parliamentarian officers who were supported by many of their troops and by a few others who joined them. A Royalist rising it was not.

However, perhaps aware that, having made war on and killed loyal Parliamentarian troops and been condemned by parliament as traitors and with further New Model units being sent against them, their only hope of survival would be to attract much wider support in a predominantly Royalist region, on 10 April Poyer and Powell issued a declaration setting out a much broader and in significant parts pro-Royalist programme. They claimed that parliament had promised that 'the true Religion should be advanced, the King made great and glorious, and the just Priviledges of Parliament, the Lawes of the Land, and the Liberty of the People maintained'. But victory in the civil war had not brought these promised fruits and instead

> the Errours of the former Government, are now so farre exceeded both in Church and Commonwealth; that they are either justified, or at least so much excused, as that it is desired by the most and best of men, rather to enjoy the former againe, then to suffer such a Reformation, wherein the Publique good is pretended, and the particular ends of the Reformers intended.

Despite the time which had passed since parliament had won the civil war, the things fought for had not come about, the authors suggested, for the King was imprisoned rather than being allowed to enter into a personal treaty with parliament, religion, laws and liberties were together 'so much trampled upon, and destroyed' and 'the greatest Tyranny and Arbitrary Power set over us, that the wit of man, or malice of the Devil can invent', all to 'satisfie the Avarice and Ambition of a few men'. The declaration highlighted alleged plans to intensify sequestration of the gentry and to extend excise and other taxes, suggested that the local agents of parliament were intending 'to bring in other Forces, such as may execute their Wils' and claimed that they also intended 'to put downe the Booke of Common-prayer in these parts, as they have already done in the rest of the Kingdome', the authors thereby indicating support for the traditional Church of England Prayer Book. They proclaimed that they were making a stand to uphold 'our first Principles', namely to 'bring the King to a Personal Treaty with his Parliament with Honour, Freedome, and Safety' in a way which would protect and preserve the 'just Prerogatives

40 *Declaration and Resolution*, p.3.

of the King', the 'Priviledges of Parliament', the laws of the land and the liberties of the people, as well as pledging to 'protect the people from Injury' and to 'maintaine the Protestant Religion, and the Common-prayer [book] as it is established by Law in this Land', to which end they 'crave[d] the Assistance of the whole Kingdome'.[41]

Making clear their change of direction, Poyer and Powell apparently sent a copy of this declaration to the Prince of Wales, with a covering undated letter emphasising that they had hitherto served parliament in the belief that it would make the King great again, but that now that they realised they had been deceived in this and that parliament was not working to that end, they were taking it upon themselves 'to serve your Royall Father, and Yourselfe, as farre as we are able, to make you both greate and glorious', claiming – perhaps spuriously – already to have contacted the King direct. They hoped that the Prince of Wales would not only endorse their stand and their programme but also take steps to supply their present 'wants and supplies'.[42] Later in April the Prince of Wales replied from the Continent, duly signifying his support for the programme and its protagonists, but providing no financial or material aid.[43] We have already noted several instances of Royalist risings and Royalist leaderships toning down their support for the King and setting out a much wider programme, pitched to attract disillusioned Parliamentarians. Here is an apparent example of the opposite, of a rising led by Parliamentarian offers and supported by hitherto Parliamentarian troops reorientating itself in order to win a broader following, including, through its new pro-Royalist statements and rhetoric, wider support across south Wales, a region of strong and popular Royalism.

While unable to provide material or military support, Prince Charles did endorse the stand being taken by Poyer and Powell and issued a commission to Laugharne to act as his general in south Wales. As a result of this, and perhaps of their 10 April *Declaration*, some of the pro-Royalist gentry of south Wales and substantial numbers of the hitherto mainly pro-Royalist population of the region threw in their lot with the leaders of the south Pembrokeshire rising.[44] That rising and the wider movement quickly unravelled, first in early May as local loyal units of the Parliamentarian army inflicted a stinging defeat on the raggle-taggle Royalist army at St Fagan's, and then when Cromwell's New Model force rolled through the region, recapturing Chepstow, Tenby and, following a lengthy siege, Pembroke.[45] But the key point is that this south-western and southern Wales arm of the second civil war appears to have originated in an anti-Parliamentarian stand taken by previously loyal Parliamentarian officers in a hitherto pro-Parliamentarian enclave, which only a good two or three months after it had begun

41 *The Declaration of Col. Poyer, and Col. Powel, and the Officers and Soldiers under their Command* (1648), pp.1–6.
42 *Colonell Powell and Col. Poyers Letter to his Highnesse the Prince of Wales* (1648), pp.3–4.
43 *A Copy of his Highnesse Prince Charles his Letter to the Commanders of his Majesties Forces* (1648), pp.1–3.
44 Bowen concludes that the *Declaration* had a strong appeal to Royalists and to somewhat disgruntled moderate former Parliamentarians on the political Presbyterian wing; he also notes that part or all of the text was circulated, sometimes in an edited or modified form – notably dropping or toning down the support for the Prayer Book and thus for the traditionalist Church of England found in the original text of 10 April in order to appeal to those who had Presbyterian religious sympathies – not only in other parts of south Wales but in other regions, including south-west England and perhaps north Wales too. Bowen, *John Poyer*, pp.133–39.
45 The unravelling of the rising from mid April onwards is the focus of Matthews, 'A Storme Out of Wales', charted in detail in chapters 2–6, and is explored more briefly in Bowen, *John Poyer*, chapter 7. Although not covered as fully as the prolonged operation against Colchester, perhaps because it was much further from the capital, Cromwell's lengthy siege of Pembroke was reported in the London press, in the weekly newspapers and in pamphlets, including *A Dangerous Fight at Pembrooke Castle, Betwixt the Forces Commanded by Lieutenant Gen. Cromwell, and the Forces Commanded by Major Gen. Langhorne and Colonel Iohn Poyer* (1648) and *A Great and Bloody Fight at Penbrook Castle* (1648).

was then broadened out and repositioned, overtly to align itself with the King's case, from this point adopting Royalist language and issues and fighting in support of the Stuarts. The obvious conclusion is that Poyer and his colleagues either, after all their years of Parliamentarianism, had suddenly become won over to Royalism through some sort of Damoclean conversion, or, more cynically but perhaps more plausibly, had decided to realign their movement once they had completely burnt their boats with parliament and in order to have any hope of survival needed to win wider support in an overwhelmingly Royalist region.

But just like the origins and development of the risings of 1648 in Kent and Essex, if we dig deeper in south Wales the story becomes more complex and the obvious interpretation may not, in fact, be the correct one. Poyer always claimed that he had not changed his principles or position and that throughout the 1640s, including during 1648, he remained true to and consistently aligned with the goals which had led him to support the Parliamentarian cause at and from the outbreak of civil war in 1642. In other words, in his eyes at least he had not moved away from his Parliamentarian principles; instead, parliament had moved away from them and thus from him. That comes across in many of the statements which Poyer issued during the early stages of the rising, before he came out for the King, such as his declaration of 13 March in which he pledged his continuing loyalty to the Solemn League and Covenant, that is to the terms of the alliance which the English parliament had concluded with the Scottish Covenanter government in summer 1643, as well as stressing that he was 'for king and parliament', not a sign of Royalism but by then a somewhat unfashionable and anachronistic use of the common Parliamentarian slogan of the main civil war.[46]

It was also very much the underlying message and thrust of the *Declaration* which Poyer and Powell issued on 10 April, their first public pronouncement containing explicitly pro-Royalist sentiments. On the title page itself, they stressed that their main goals of spring 1648, 'Restoring His Majesty to His just Prerogative, and the Lawes to their due Course, for the maintenance of the Protestant Religion, and the Liberty of the Subject', were precisely 'the Ground[s] of their first taking up Armes' in 1642. As the text unfolded, they reiterated that their own views on religion, liberty and monarchy had not changed and that instead it was the Long Parliament and its agents who had not stood by and fulfilled the Parliamentarian objectives of the early 1640s, even though they had secured military victory and taken control of the King several years before. 'Although our Party have prevailed almost these three yeeres, and the King in the power of the Reformers almost these two yeeres; yet the things promised to be reformed, and which wee fought for, are scarce so much entered into, or debated, but cleare contrary things now acted'. They claimed that their stance was motivated by their continuing adherence to religion, the law, liberty and a just settlement with the King, objectives which parliament had initially supported but had since moved away from and betrayed, in the process setting up tyranny and arbitrary power. Worse was to come, Poyer and Powell alleged, in terms of the mistreatment of the gentry, the extension of direct and indirect taxes and the destruction of the Prayer Book. That is why, they asserted, they were now compelled to make a stand in support of their 'first Principles'; 'wee doe still continue to our first Principles'.[47]

While there might be a degree of self-deception in all this to explain and excuse their apparent desertion of the Parliamentarian cause, Bowen sees considerable justification in Poyer's self-appraisal. He notes that while he had been loyal to parliament during the main civil war, the evidence suggests that he had always been on the moderate or 'political-Presbyterian' wing, and also that while he was

---

46 Poyer, *Declaration and Resolution*, p.4; see also Bowen, *John Poyer*, p.120.
47 *Declaration of Col. Poyer, and Col. Powel*, pp.1–6. The text is discussed by Bowen, *John Poyer*, pp.131–33.

strongly anti-Catholic, he had also shown consistent support for the Church of England and its Prayer Book. Indeed, Bowen suggests that one of Poyer's problems, especially in 1648, was that he was too consistent to his original (in 1642 Parliamentarian) principles, to the point of inflexibility, in contrast to his leading opponents in Pembrokeshire of the later 1640s, who had proved very adept at moving with the shifting tides.[48]

Had space permitted, this chapter could have ranged geographically more widely and examined some of the other outbursts of 1648; for example, those occurring at Norwich around Easter-time, in western Cornwall during the latter half of May, in Surrey in early July, ending in a pursuit of the protagonists northwards as far as Huntingdonshire, and in Herefordshire in late July and August, all generated contemporary coverage and source material which are suggestive and repay close examination.[49] However, enough has been said about the two main home-grown risings of 1648, the focus of this chapter, to permit some broader conclusions to be drawn about their origins and nature.

Robert Ashton's reappraisal of the origins of the second civil war in his major study of 1994, together with the key conclusions Brian Lyndon presented in a clutch of articles of the early and mid 1980s, and encapsulated in the closing chapter of John Morrill's *Revolt in the Provinces* in which in 1999 he revisited and revised some of his earlier findings, together make a substantial case for seeing the events of 1648 (and the preceding protests and petitions of 1647, too) as elements of wider and often quite organised and well-supported expressions of disappointment and disaffection with Parliamentarian rule, policies and (local) personnel in the later 1640s, some of which led on to armed and violent outbursts, though much of which did not. That was overlain by a second factor, the activities of clear and longstanding Royalists, who sought to use this wider anti-Parliamentarian but not particularly pro-Royalist – beyond a broad wish to see the King treated respectfully and included in a negotiated new settlement – discontent for their own ends, infiltrating and exploiting it to achieve their goals, of rebuilding royal power and restoring Charles I to something much closer to his traditional kingship and more or less full prerogative powers. In the end, many such Royalist attempts failed to progress, because, even when artfully played down or disguised, their real objectives were too different from those of the disillusioned Parliamentarians and non-Royalists and, though a few did progress as far as armed risings, they were weakened by the resulting fracture lines and incongruities within them.[50]

That pattern and interpretation works well for the course of events in Kent and Essex. As we have seen, the Kentish rebellion did not originate in explicit Royalism, more a mixture of localism, traditionalism and antagonism towards parliament and its agents, but it was taken over by an overtly Royalist leadership who pursued a programme which was at heart Royalist, though in their public and published documents they disguised or concealed their support for the King and instead highlighted a range of other grievances and goals in an attempt to win broader support. The Essex phase, too, began

---

48   A point made several times by Bowen, *John Poyer*, including in his preface at p.4.
49   In a brief section towards the end of his book, 'Insurgent war aims', Ashton cites the Herefordshire venture as a further prime examples of a rising in which from the outset and throughout leadership rested with established Royalists ('Cavalier' is Ashton preferred term) but, realising that if they 'were to have any prospect of recruiting sizable numbers of' alienated Parliamentarians, 'they obviously needed to tone down extreme Cavalier sentiments and to stress considerations such as the regime's unconstitutional excesses, inordinate cost, and shocking violations of traditional liberties'; he contrasts this with the leadership of the Surrey rising, which included a formerly quite active Parliamentarian peer, seeing the stress they put in their public declarations on restoring the King only with limited and balanced constitutional powers as 'for once' therefore credible and genuine. Ashton, *Counter Revolution*, pp.449–50.
50   Ashton, *Counter Revolution, passim*.; Lyndon, 'Essex and the king's cause in 1648', 'Parliament's army in Essex, 1648' and 'The South and the start of the second civil war'; Morrill, *Revolt of the Provinces*, pp.204–8.

with a mutiny by Parliamentarian officers, provoked by grievances over their treatment, and apparently not by any overtly Royalist sentiments, feeding into wider disillusionment within the county, but again such origins were quickly overwhelmed and lost as the rebellion was taken over and led by a body of old and well-established Royalists, acting in support of the King.

Conversely, that pattern and interpretation work far less well when applied to the Pembrokeshire rising.[51] It not only began as, but also for many weeks, even months, it remained, a Parliamentarian mutiny, a rising led by loyal and long-serving Parliamentarian army officers, provoked by what they viewed as their harsh treatment by parliament and its agents and by the military high command. Only much later, when faced with parliament's intransigence and military response, did the leaders of the mutiny consciously widen their programme and their goals, seeking to make contact with the King and the Prince of Wales and embracing some elements of Royalism in an attempt to win Royalist support. That tactic worked fairly well in Glamorganshire, encouraging many old Royalists to take up arms – though those men never assumed the leadership, as they did in Kent and in the long Colchester phase of the Essex rising – but less so in southern Pembrokeshire and neighbouring parts of Carmarthenshire, where Royalism was probably less strong on the ground and where prominent old Royalist gentry generally remained aloof. While old Royalists might with some success rebrand their movement to attract anti-Parliamentarian sentiment, the attempt by old Parliamentarians to rebrand their movement to attract old Royalists was perhaps less effective. In any case, however, the support for the King's cause apparent in and expressed by Poyer, Powell and Laugharne from 10 April onwards was almost certainly a much more moderate and conditional form of Royalism – in Poyer's case, emerging from a long-standing and fairly consistent set of objectives which had for many years made him a Parliamentarian – rather than the harder-core Royalism of Norwich, Loughborough and Capel and of many of the armed men they attracted to them.

This tale of two risings has sought to demonstrate that it is often hard to find the true roots and origins of some of the violent outbursts of 1648 and that, when seeking to unravel and discern whether they were at heart or predominantly pro-Royalist or anti-Parliamentarian in nature, the obvious and apparent answers may not, in fact, be the correct ones; digging deeper often leads to more opaque, ambiguous or nuanced answers. It has also shown that the Kent and Essex rising on the one hand and the Pembrokeshire and south Wales rising on the other not only shared some common factors but also in other ways could appear to be the reverse of each other – the former pro-Royalist from the outset but seemingly realigned to attract support from disgruntled Parliamentarians in a hitherto strongly pro-Parliamentarian region, the latter anti-parliament at the outset and for a long while but then seemingly realigned to attract support from old Royalists in a region which had been dominated by elite and popular Royalism. However, in both cases it has been demonstrated that in fact things are not so clear or all that they might seem and that that interpretation needs to be modified in key areas. Lastly, what we might call the Lyndon thesis works well for the Kent and Essex outbursts, most notably in the lead-up to the engagement at Maidstone and through the Colchester phase, though it is not such a good fit for the developments in southern Pembrokeshire and further afield in south Wales and seems to underplay the distinctiveness of the events there.

---

51 Lyndon's coverage of the Pembrokeshire and south Wales rising is probably the least convincing part of his article 'The South and the start of the second civil war', pp.396–97, or, more fairly, it is the part which has most been overtaken by fuller work on the extant primary sources and by the more detailed published research which has appeared since he wrote his paper.

Three Armies into One? Scottish Engager Military Organisation in 1648

Edward M. Furgol

On 26 December 1647 (after 19 months of negotiations), three Scottish nobles signed a treaty with Charles I, requiring them to mobilise a Scottish army. The objectives were to defeat the New Model Army in England and to free Charles I. They had at their disposal two armies – one of over 3,000 men in Ulster and another in Scotland of about 7,000 men and needed to produce a parliamentary act of levy for a third. Uniting these forces would theoretically give the Scottish Engagers the military strength to gain their objectives. On 21 January 1648 news of the Engagement arrived in Edinburgh; Between 10 and 15 February the Committee of Estates was briefed about the document and accepted it as government policy. Although the Scottish Parliament began meeting on 4 March, the Engagers did nothing until 18 April when they created new shire committees or committees of war. The situation accelerated on the 28th when English Royalist Sir Marmaduke Langdale occupied Berwick; the next day his compatriot Sir Philip Musgrave occupied Carlisle. Still, the Engagers remained inactive. The Engagers managed to keep their opponents in the kirk in check until 28 April, when the Commission of the General Assembly issued a lengthy protest against the Engagement. The Engagers' inaction had lost them two and a half precious months during which the kirk offered no opposition. They could and should have used the Committee of Estates' authority to issue recruiting warrants for existing units to bring them to full strength (7,410 men) and reinforce them.[1] For cavalry, particularly, which cannot train on the march, recruiting men in February to April would have proven especially beneficial.

Finally, on 4 May the Estates passed an act of levy for 27,750 foot and 2,160 horse, setting rendezvouses in the shires for 24 or 27 May. That was an extremely ambitious deadline and one unlikely to be met even with perfect coordination. Earlier in the decade (between 26 November 1643 and 19 January 1644), a united Covenanter movement had taken 54 days to levy 18,000 foot and 3,000 horse and dragoons. The new levy was 42 percent greater than the earlier one. In 1648 the usual Covenanter coordination for levying men between the national government, local authorities and the church fractured, when the last objected to the treaty's clause establishing Presbyterianism in England and Ireland for only three years. For nine years, the Covenanters had an established levying system relying on the coordination of national and local governments and the church. The national authority selected the

---

1   For mid-1640 examples of the Committee of Estates issuing orders for reinforcing existing units see, *At Stirling the 12. of June 1645* (Edinburgh: 1645), s.s.; *Act anent recruiting the armies* (Edinburgh: 1646), 2–4. For the church's protest see, *The Records of the Commissioners of the General Assemblies of the Church of Scotland, 1646–52*, 3 vols., eds. J.D. Marwick and J. Christie (Scottish Historical Society, 1892–1909), I. 528–31.

colonels and assigned one or more shires the quota for each regiment/unit. The county committee of the shire or committee of war set local quotas. The county's presbyteries informed its ministers and elders to publicise the levy. In the parishes, ministers, elders, and heritors listed the fencible men – those aged 16–60 – then selected recruits. The parish ministers preached sermons supporting the levy. The kirk session and the burghs also apprehended evaders, and deserters/runaways, returning them to the colours. To assist the effort the Estates adjourned from 11 May to 1 June.

Resistance to the levy varied by county, but nationally only 10.3 percent of the 1,000 ministers supported it. That meant potential recruits had a far greater chance of hearing that service in the army endangered their souls as opposed to serving as loyal subjects saving the King. Locally, south of the Firth of Tay the anti-Engager kirk party predominated in the synods, presbyteries, and many parishes. In some shires the kirk party also controlled the committee of war. That was the case across the southwest Lowlands in the shires of Ayr, Dumfries, Dunbarton, Kirkcudbright, Lanark, Renfrew and Wigton, and also in the eastern Lowlands in East Lothian and Fife or in nine of the thirty-three shires. Thus, the usual organisational support for a national levy disintegrated. Experienced men refused to set quotas and recruit; the ministers condemned any who joined the regiments as enemies of religion.[2] These counties accounted for 5,150 soldiers or 18.5 percent of the foot levy and 940 troopers or 43.5 percent of the horse levy.[3] In addition, a quarter of the Engager Army colonels had no experience in the Covenanter levy process, which was partly due to the refusal of 10 Scottish New

---

2   For sermons against the levy, *The Diplomatic Correspondence of Jean de Montereul and the Brothers de Bellièvre, French Ambassadors to England and Scotland 1645–48*, 2 vols., ed. J.G. Fotheringham (Scottish History Society, 1 Ser., xxix–xxx, 1898), II. 482, 492; *The Memoirs of Henry Guthry, late bishop of Dunkeld*, ed. G. Crawfurd (Glasgow: 1748), 274; W. Makey 'Ministers in Scottish parishes, 1648' (unpublished), 105.

3   All levy quota numbers are from *The Acts of the Parliament of Scotland (APS)*, 12 vols., eds. T. Thomson and C. Innes (Edinburgh: 1814–75), VI, I. 54–5. Ayrshire: anti-Engager petitions – committee of war, National Library of Scotland, Wodrow Analecta MS. Folio 20, f. 59; National Records of Scotland, PR Ayr, 17.5.1648; levy quotas: 80 horse, Renfrewshire 1,000 foot and 120 horse. Dumfriesshire: anti-Engager petitions – Dumfries burgh Stevenson, 'The Battle of Mauchline Moor 1648, *Ayrshire Collections*, XI (1973), 4; PR Dumfries, *Historical Manuscript Commission*, LXXII, 231; levy quotas: 1,200 foot and 80 horse; Dunbartonshire: anti-Engager petition -- PR Dunbarton, 16.5.1648; levy quota: 40 horse; Stewartry of Kirkcudbright: anti-Engager petition – committee of war, Stevenson, 'Mauchline Moor', 4; levy quota: 80 horse with Wigtonshire; Lanarkshire: anti-Engager petitions –committee of war, Stevenson, 'Mauchline Moor', 4; Glasgow burgh, *Glasgow*, 133–4; NRS, PR Biggar ff177–8, 196; PR Lanark *HMC*, LXXII, 234; NRS, PR Glasgow III. 106–8 with parishes of Barony kirk, Cader, Carank, Govan, Lequham, Monydie, Rutherglen; NRS PR Glasgow III. 101–5; levy quotas: 1,200 foot and 180 horse; Renfrewshire: anti-Engager petitions – committee of war, Stevenson, 'Mauchline Moor', 4; NRS, PR Paisley 25.5.1648 and all kirk session, NRS PR Paisley, 25.5.1648; levy quota: 80 horse and see Ayrshire above; Wigtonshire: anti-Engager petitions – committee of war, Stevenson, 'Mauchline Moor', 4; NRS, PR Stranraer I. f. 136; levy quota: 40 horse; East Lothian: anti-Engager petitions – committee of war, *APS*, VI, I. 691; NRS, PR Haddington 7.6.1648; Dunbar and Haddington presbyteries, *APS*, VI, I. 691; levy quotas: 1,200 foot and 80 horse; Fife: anti-Engager petitions – committee of war, *HMC*, LXXII, 235; NRS, PR Dunfermline I. f.40, Kirkcaldy presbytery, *HMC*, LXXII, 236; St. Andrews presbytery, *Selections from the minutes of the Presbyteries of St. Andrews and Cupar, 1641–49*, ed. G.R. Kinloch (Abbotsford Club, VII, 1837), 41; NRS, KSR Anstruther Easter, 30.5.1648; KSR Falkland I. f. 74; KSR Kingsbarns, I. f. 18; levy quotas: 750 foot with Kinross-shire and 160 horse. For meeting the levy quotas by quartering in Glasgow and Renfrew, *The Letters and Journals of Robert Baillie, Principal of the University of Glasgow, 1637–1662*, ed. D. Laing (Bannatyne Club, LXXII, parts I–II, LXXVII, 1841–42), III. 47–8; J. Turner, *Memoirs of His Own Life and Times, 1632–1670*, ed. T. Thomson (Bannatyne Club, XXVIII, 1829), 53–5; and by seizing men during church services, *Selections from the Registers of the Presbytery of Lanark, 1623–1709*, ed., J. Robertson (Abbotsford Club, XVI, 1839), 60–1.

Model Army commanders to resign in 1648. Even forcing out recruits by quartering or taking men from their beds led to filling only half of the levy quotas (A peculiarity of the act of levy for horse regiments was that they required only 155 men in two troops or 180 in three unlike the regiments of the Army of the Solemn League and Covenant that had 600 men in eight troops. That tripled the number of staff officers, increasing the financial requirements to command the same number of men. Perhaps the Engager leaders thought financial inducements might increase support). Little wonder that on 8 July (66 days after the act of levy) when Lord General the Duke of Hamilton led his men into England to protect Sir Marmaduke Langdale's 3,000–4,000 men from Major General John Lambert's section of the New Model Army, he had only 7,000 foot and 3,500 horse.[4] Reinforcements later increased the army by 3,000 foot and perhaps another 500 horse. Contrary to Hamilton's hopes no Lancastrian Presbyterians joined him due to the Church of Scotland's open and constant opposition.[5]

What was the balance between veterans and recruits in that army? From the Scottish New Model Army units, whose men had been under the colours for three–five years, it had notionally 3,200 veteran foot in four regiments and 375 veteran horse with 220 recruits in five regiments. The Engagers ordered Stewart's/Ludovick Leslie's Foot to garrison Berwick, reducing the experienced foot by a quarter.[6] Kirk party loyalty meant two generals, eight colonels, three lieutenant colonels and a major were missing; Holburn's/Turner's Foot lost not only its colonel and lieutenant colonel, but also most of the subalterns.[7] What happened to the rest of the Scottish New Model?

Some in the Engager regime feared more for their position in Scotland than valued achieving their objectives in England. The committee of war and kirk anti-Engager petitions persuaded Lord General Hamilton's brother, the Earl of Lanark, that troops must remain in Scotland until they had secured internal order. Lauderdale, another leading Engager, although a diplomat, considered *immediate* military success in England of paramount importance (his views mirrored Lord General Leven's in 1644–46 that England was the critical theatre of operations for the Covenanters. Events confirmed Lauderdale's analysis for between 28 April and 8 July the English New Model Army operated in three non-supporting divisions, inviting defeat in detail). Desertion by kirk party soldiers, the refusal of the Marquis of Argyll's and Campbell of Ardkinglas' Highland Foot regiments (and possibly Riccarton's Horse Troop)[8] to accept Engager orders, as well as a kirk party gathering at Mauchline Moor in Ayrshire led the Engagers to follow Lanark's desire.[9] The 12 June defeat of those on Mauchline Moor and the subsequent inaction of the Highland regiments failed to calm Lanark's apprehensions.

---

4   NRS, KSR Linlithgow, –. 32v; 'A Declaration from Scotland concerning the Advance of the Scots Army: Who are come into England; (London: 1648), in *Reprints of Rare Tracts Chiefly Illustrative of the History of the Northern counties*, 3 vols., ed. M.A. Richardson (Newcastle: 1845–49), II. 150 (10–11 in original); J. Turner, *Memoirs of his own life and times* (Edinburgh, 1829), 53–5, 57.
5   Turner, *Memoirs*, 62.
6   NRS, PA. 15.10, 2; *APS*, VI, I. 673, 684, 698; NRS, PA, VI, I. 98.
7   Turner, *Memoirs*, 53. F, *RH*.
8   NRS, B.6.182., 27v; PA. 7.4, 21; PA. 15.10, 1, 10; PR Ayr, 2 March 1648; PR Dunblane, 21 February 1649; *APS*, VI, I. 672–4, 683, 719; *APS*, VI, II. 21–2, 92, 98; *C.J.*, VI. 685; *Edinburgh*, 109–11; *Memoirs of Guthry*, 240, 278–9, *Muniments of the Royal Burgh of Irvine*, 3 vols. (Ayrshire and Galloway Arch. Assoc, 1890–91), II. 73; *Three Letters*, 5; Turner, *Memoirs*, 52; Reid, *Scots Colours*, 12–3; B. Robertson, *Lordship and Power in the North of Scotland: The Noble House of Huntly 1603–1690* (Edinburgh: 2011), 143; Stevenson, *Alasdair*, 231–40.
9   D. Stevenson, *Revolution and Counter-Revolution in Scotland 1644–1651* (London: 1977), 109–11. A third infantry regiment, Lawers' Foot from the Ulster Army (serving in Scotland from 1644), only entered England, but did not march into Lancashire before returning to Scotland, E.M. Furgol, *A Regimental History of the Covenanting Armies 1639–1651* (Edinburgh: 1990), 91.

Fear of fellow Scots convinced the Engagers to leave sizeable forces in Scotland. They included the following veterans: 179 dragoons (in two companies with 34 attached to a cavalry regiment), one regiment of 800 foot, and 10 cavalry units (nine regiments and a troop) of 750 long-serving horse plus 800 recruits, depriving Hamilton of 1,729 veterans and 800 raw cavalry.[10] In addition to that depletion of the main army, the Engagers withheld new recruits from it. Initially, they retained 18 dragoons, 2,000 foot and 1,260 horse.[11] Those decisions meant Hamilton faced the English New Model Army with about 5,800 fewer men than he could have had (on 31 July, the Engagers ordered a further levy of 1,369 cavalry to be made into three 456-man horse regiments for internal security. In August they authorised the raising of 3,000 Highlanders for the same purpose. Those acts created a home army of about 10,000 men[12]). When one adds Callendar's Foot, garrisoning Carlisle, and Ludovick's Leslie's Foot in Berwick[13] the reduction rises to about 7,600 men. Therefore, the Engagers' main strike force lost both veterans and bodies by ignoring the priority of England.

What happened with the other source of veterans – the Ulster Army? It had over 3,000 foot in seven regiments and four horse troops (an eighth foot regiment – Lawers' is discussed below). On 7 April, the Ulster Army council of war offered the Engagers troops to invade England. Negotiations between the council and Estates proceeded in May. The council agreed to provide 2,100 foot (taking 300 men

---

10 These units included: Foot regiment: Pitscottie's/ Toures' (800), Horse regiments (veteran and recruit numbers in parentheses): Aldie's (75 and 80), D. Barclay's (75 horse and 70 dragoons plus 80 recruits), H. Barclay's (75 and 80), Fraser's (75 and 80), Ker's/ Ramsay's (75 and 105), Lockhart's (75 and 110), Ludquharn's (75 and 80), Middleton's (75 and 80), Montgomery's/ Viscount Montgomery's (75 and 160), Murray's (75 and 80), Strachan's (75 and 80); Horse troops: Bogie's (75), Brown's/ Earl of Callendar's (75 and 30); Dragoon companies: Blair's (34), Leslie's/ Ferguson/s (70), Sharp's/ D. Barclay's (70), NLS, Dep. 175, Box 67, 647; Wodrow Analecta Folio 63, 74; NRS, GD. 38.1, 193; KSR Duffus, I. 67; PA. 15.10, 2, 4–9, 11; PR Elgin, I. 279; TNA, SP 41/2, 164–99; *APS*, VI, I. 623, 673–4, 684–6, 698,709, 719; *APS*, VI, II. 56, 56, 62, 74, 98, 122; G. Burnet, *The Memoirs of the Lives and actions of James and William, dukes of Hamilton and Castle-Herald* (2nd edn., Oxford: 1852), 428; 'A Declaration from Scotland Concerning the Advance of the Scots Army: Who are Come into England' (London: 1648), in *Reprints of Rare Tracts Chiefly Illustrative of the Northern counties*, 3 vols, ed. M.A. Richardson (Newcastle: 1845–9), II. 10; Gordon, *Short Abridgement*, 211; *Hist. MSS. Comm.* llth Rep. pt. I. 87; *Memoirs of Guthry*, 240; *The Miscellany of the Spalding Club*, vol. 3, ed. J. Stuart (Spalding Club, XVI, 1846), 199–200; *RCGA*, II. 170; *RCGA*, III. 156; Turner, *Memoirs*, 47, 49, 52, 58, 74, 76; Foster, *Members*, 52, 356; R. Gordon and G. Gordon, *A Geneaological History of the Earldom of Sutherland* (Edinburgh: 1813), 542; *Scots Peerage*, VI. 184; Woolrych, *Battles*, 164, 167, 175–7, 179; SSNE 1348, 1851, 1933, 2920, 3472, 8050.
11 Foot regiment: Earl of Glencairn's (levy quota 1,000), Earl of Morton's (levy quota 1,000), *APS*, VI, II. 55; *Charters and Other Records of the City and Royal Burgh of Kirkwall*, ed. J Mooney (Kirkwall: 1950), 86–7; *RCGA*, II. 66; *RCGA*, III. 272, Paterson, *Ayr*, I. 163; *Scots Peerage*, IV. 247–8. Horse regiments: Earl of Crawford-Lindsay's, Garthland's, Home's, Innes', Earl of Lanark's, and Lord Sinclair's, NRS, KSR Dundonald, I. 38v; KSR Gargunnock, I. 45; PR Elgin, I. 252; PR Stranraer, I. 179v; NLS, Dep. 175, Box 67, 609, 633; *APS*, VI, II. 55–6, 62, 736; Guthry, 285; Kirkcaldie, 328; *RCGA*, II. 47–8, 66, 187, 195, 309, 313; *Selections from the Minutes of the Presbyteries of St. Andrews and Cupar, 1641–48*, ed. G.R. Kinloch (Abbotsford Club, VIIi, 1837), 61; 'Unpublished papers of John Seventh Lord Sinclair, Covenanter and Royalist', ed. J.A. Fairley, *Trans. Buchan Field Club*, VIII (1904–5), 149, 151; Foster, *Members*, 225; R. Gordon and G. Gordon, *A Geneaological History of the Earldom of Sutherland* (Edinburgh: 1813), 42; Paterson, *Ayr*, I. 163; *Scots Peerage*, III. 35–6; *Scots Peerage*, IV. 379; *Scots Peerage*, VII. 576; Stevenson, *Covenanters*, 258–60.
12 NRS, PA. 7.23/2.37 ; *Act for a new levie of horse to be put out by the shires: And list of the colonels and the their inferiour officers, with their severall numbers of horse* (Edinburgh: 164), 4; Stevenson, *Revolution*, 113.
13 *APS*, VI, II. 55, 115; 'A Declaration from Scotland concerning the Advance of the Scots Army: Who are come into England' (London: 1648) in *Reprints of Rare Tracts Chiefly Illustrative of the History of the Northern counties*, 3 vols., ed. M. A. Richardson (Newcastle: 1845–49), II. 11; *Baillie*, III. 48–9; Turner, *Memoirs*, 56, 58.

from each regiment), and 1,500 horse (with most of them to be raised by Colonel George Monro, with the help of Ulster Scots Sir Frederick Hamilton and Sir Robert Stewart). To secure that force the Engagers paid the army between £72,000 and £108,000 Scots in arrears. Glencairn's Foot, despite its colonel's loyalty to the Engagement, supported the kirk party so vehemently that the council ejected it from the army on 27 June and took no drafts from it. By 31 July only 1,500 veteran foot and 400 horse or 53 percent of the plan force had arrived in northwestern England and southwestern Scotland (the English parliamentarian navy and Argyll's frigate had intercepted and returned at least 300 infantry). At a meeting in Kendal in early August George Monro's Ulster Force became independent of the duke of Hamilton's army in England. The situation arose because Monro would only acceptance Hamilton's direct orders and not those of his Lieutenant Generals Callendar and Middleton. Hamilton excused the further diminution of his army by stating Monro's force would escort the expected – but never arriving – train of artillery and reinforcements.[14] Hamilton's and Lanark's decisions had caused the strike force to lose 4,400 veterans and 3,260 levies for a total of nearly 7,700 men. Hamilton's army probably had 10,000 foot and 4,000 horse at its greatest strength[15]. The additional 10,000 plus men would have increased it by 70 percent to 24,000 men. With Langdale's 3,000 men that army would have given even Cromwell, with about 9,000 troops, pause before attacking.

By mid-August, the Engagers had six forces. They were: the remnant of the army in Ulster, Lanark's security force in Scotland, two garrisons in England, Monro's Ulster force including Lawers' Foot – a unit that marched with the Engagers until 10–19 September, Hamilton's-Baillie's foot command and Callendar's-Middleton's cavalry command. Langdale's independent command continued to exist. Rather than establishing local dominance in northwest England and defeating Lambert's force, Hamilton's immobility for a month had given time for Cromwell's contingent from southwest Wales

---

14   NRS, PA. 7.6, 154, 295; PR Perth, III. 180; Adair, *Narrative*, 149, 167; G. Burnet, *The Lives and actions of James and William, dukes of Hamilton and Castle-Herald* (2nd edn., Oxford: 1852), 453; 'Declaration from Scotland', II. 11; 'Duke of Hamilton's Expedition to England 1648', ed. C.H. Firth, *Miscellany of the Scottish History Society*, II (Scot. His. Soc., 1st Ser., XLIV, 1904), 310; Turner, *Memoirs*, 59, suggested General of Artillery Alexander Hamilton was too senile to organise a train of artillery; Stevenson, *Covenanters*, 260–2, 269–77; SSNE, 3119, 3834; Woolrych, *Battles*, 161–2, 164–5, 180–1. Lieutenant Colonel William Borthwick of Lindsay's Foot in the Ulster Army, who had persuaded that army's council of war to accept the Engagement, probably served in the unit. His excommunication as an Engager was announced in Elie on 17 December 1648 along with that of a Captain [William] Morton (Myrton) of Lindsay's. On 23 January 1651, the Commission sent him to St. Andrews presbytery to repent for his role in the Engagement and to swear the Solemn League and Covenant; he was received in Elie on 16 February. NRS, KSR Elie, I. 177, 214; *RCGA*, III. 258–9.
15   Burnet, *Lives*, 451.

to join Lambert setting the scene for a series of English New Model victories at Preston[16], Winwick[17], Warrington[18], and Uttoxeter.[19]

The Engagers' situation in Scotland underwent a similar decline, despite the troops retained there and their reinforcement by units retreating from England. In mid-August, the Engagers had over 4,500 troops in Scotland. Later in the month kirk party stalwarts (called Whigs, leading the rebellion to be called the Whiggamore Raid), in Ayrshire and Lanarkshire revolted. Major General Robert Montgomery led them to victory in a Lanarkshire skirmish. Then Monro's force with fragments of Hamilton's army united with Lanark's force in Midlothian. The Engagers moved north toward Stirling. The raiders took Edinburgh on 28 August, then its castle on 5 September. Despite victories at Linlithgow (11 September) and against Argyll at Stirling (on the 12th), the Engager situation deteriorated. On the 12th Fife and Borders reinforcements joined the raiders at Falkirk and between the 10th and 19th Lawers' defected. Then Cromwell's army entered Scotland on the 21st. Fighting

---

16   Lord Cochrane's Foot, *APS*, VI. II. 55; Furgol, *Regimental history*, 272; J. Paterson, *History of the county of Ayr*, 2 vols. (Edinburgh: 1847), I. 163; Kelhead's Foot, which defended the Ribble bridge, *A Letter From Edinburgh Containing a true and perfite Relation of all the Passages and Proceedings of the late Army* (n.p., 1648), C2-D. It ceased to exist before the Engager foot surrendered at Warrington. Pitscottie's/ Toures' and Earl of Roxborough's Foot formed a brigade that covered Langdale's retreat, *A Letter From Edinburgh*, C.

17   Foot regiments engaged: Earl of Atholl's, Lord Barganie's, Douglas', Duke of Hamilton's, Earl of Home's, Keith's, Earl of Kellie's, Machanie's, Maule's, Philorth's, Roxborough's, Earl of Tullibardine's, Lord Yester's, *APS*, VI, II. 54–6; Furgol, *Regimental history*, 268–9, 274, 276, 278–81, 283–4, 286–9; Reid, *Scots Colours*, 15; Woolrych, *Battles*, 169. Kelhead's and Pitscottie's/ Toures' may have been destroyed at Winwick since none of their personnel surrendered at Warrington. The destruction of the latter is not surprising since its brigade partner – Roxborough's only had 0.36 percent of its levy quota at Warrington.

18   Bold indicates veteran unit. Foot surrendered with the number of officers and men: **Marquis of Argyll's Highland Foot** (15 in one company), Earl of Atholl's (168 in seven companies), Lord Barganie's (90 in two companies), Lord Carnegie's (159 in six companies), Douglas' (142 in 10 companies), Earl of Dumfries' (57 in five companies), Gray's (37 in two companies), Duke of Hamilton's (397 in 10 companies), **Hamilton's/ General of Artillery's** (54 in three companies), Holburn's/Turner's (112 in four companies), Earl of Home's (277 in seven companies), Keith's (143 in five companies), Earl of Kellie's (110 in four companies), Machanie's (110 in five companies), Maule's (129 in four companies), Philorth's (160 in two companies), Earl of Roxborough's (36 in two to three companies), **Scott's/Baillie's** (131 in three companies), Earl of Tullibardine's (133 in six companies), Lord Yester's (81 men in nine companies), NRS, PA. 15.10, 2; *Baillie*, III. 457; A. Fraser, *The Frasers of Philorth*, 3 vols. (Edinburgh: 1879), I. 176; *Kirkcaldie*, 368; *Three Letters*,1, 3–6; Turner, *Memoirs*, 53–5, 58–9, 61, 66–7, 70, 72–7 ; W. Wheatly, *A Declaration of the Scottish Armie concerning their immediate marching towards the Borders of England* (London: 1647), 5; W. Gordon, *The History of the . . . Family of Gordon*, 2 vols. (Edinburgh: 1727), II. 558; SSNE 63; R.A. Hay, *Geneaologie of the Hayes of Tweeddale* (Edinburgh: 1835), 27, 29; Reid, *Scots Colours*, 12–23, 25, 27–35, 37; A. Woolrych, *Battles of the English Civil War* (paperback edn., London: 1966), 164–5, 172–4, 177–8. About 17 percent of the levy quotas of the foot regiments reached Warrington. Horse: Earl of Dalhousie's, *APS*, VI, II. 56; *Three Letters*, 1.

19   Horse surrendered after Warrington Bridge and at Uttoxeter: College of Justice, Lord Cranston's, Viscount Frendraught's, Duke of Hamilton's Guard, Earl Marischal's, Earl of Traquair's, Urry's, NLS, Wodrow Analecta Folio 63, 74; NRS, PA, 15.10, 4, 7; *APS*, VI, I. 674, 719; NRS, PA, II. 55–6, 122; NRS, PA, VII, 236–7; G. Burnet, *The Memoirs of the Lives and actions of James and William, dukes of Hamilton and Castle-Herald* (2nd edn., Oxford: 1852), 428; Gordon, *Short Abridgement*, 210; *RCGA*, III. 161; *Memoirs of Guthry*, 240; *Three Letters*, 1; Turner, *Memoirs*, 49, 52, 57, 65, 76; Gordon, *Family of Gordon*, II. 563; *Scots Peerage*, II. 595–6; *Scots Peerage*, IV. 377–8; *Scots Peerage*, VI. 57–9; SSNE 1348; Woolrych, *Battles*, 179. The following horse regiments probably served in England and disintegrated or surrendered there: Earl of Buchan's, Colinton's, Viscount Dudhope's, Earl of Dunfermline's, Earl of Erroll's, Viscount Kenmure's, Earl of Lauderdale's, NRS, OPR Largo, 23 December 1650; *APS*, VI, II. 56; *Government of Scotland*, 69; *RCGA*, III. 74, 94, 136, 170, 315–6, 420; *Presbyteries of St. Andrews and Cupar*, 163; *Scots Peerage*, V. 120–2, 303.

ceased and negotiations (14–26 September) ended in the Treaty of Stirling and Edinburgh (27th), leading to the Engagers' disbanding, their evacuation of Berwick and Carlisle (on 1 October) and Cromwell's departure. The Engagers' forces in northern Scotland disbanded by 10 October.[20] By then Monro's Ulster Force had disintegrated through desertion and mobbing by the local population during its march to embark for Ulster. The retention of troops in Scotland had not only weakened Hamilton's army – leading to critical mission failure, but the policy had also failed to preserve the Engager regime.

In the short term the kirk party had other successes. On 16 September, the officers of Glencairn's Foot helped New Model Colonel George Monck take Carrickfergus. Belfast and Coleraine also fell, ending the existence of the Ulster Army. For solidifying its control in Scotland, the kirk party had the two Highland Foot regiments from the Scottish New Model Army, Lawers' Foot from the Ulster army and from the Whiggamore Raid the Edinburgh (later Pitscottie's) and John Innes' Foot regiments. On 14 October 1648, the Kirk Party augmented that force with an act of levy, which gave new commands to seven officers who had refused Engager commands. In August 1649, using Ulster Army kirk partymen the Estates established the Irish Foot (later His Majesty's Lifeguard of Foot) of 396 men and an Irish Horse Troop (40 troopers plus officers).[21]

The Engager's sloth and difficulty in raising troops, Lanark's retention of veterans and new recruits to face potential internal enemies in Scotland, the decision to place strong garrisons in Berwick and Carlisle, and the failure to unite the Ulster Army contingent with Hamilton's Army contributed to a situation that made achieving the objectives of freeing the king and destroying the New Model Army nearly impossible. The Engagers' inaction and questionable decisions exacerbated an already challenging situation regarding the New Model Army that required the maximum number of troops – veteran and raw. The Engagers themselves laid the foundations for their tactical defeats and consequent strategic failure.

---

20 The forces in northern Scotland included infantry regiments: Lemlair's (levy quota 800), Earl of Moray's (levy quota 1,500), Earl of Seaforth's (levy quota 800), and a Dragoon regiment: Earl of Seaforth's (levy quota 300), NRS, PA. 7.23/2, 7, 57; PA. 11.6, 6; NLS, MS. 2961, 131; *APS*, VI, II. 55; *Government of Scotland*, 65. *The Sutherland Book*, 3 vols., ed. W. Fraser (Edinburgh: 1894), I. 249; A. Mackenzie, *History of Clan Mackenzie* (Inverness: 1879), 193–4, 204; *Scots Peerage*, VII. 508.

21 *Act for leavying of some forces for securing the peace of the kingdom untill the meeting of the Parliament* (Edinburgh, 1648), 2–5.

The Control of Command in the British Wars 1642–1651

Malcolm Wanklyn

Setting the Scene

In a recent review of a book discussing the relationship between generals and their political masters since the Korean War the issue of who was actually in charge is described as an age-old question.[1] The root cause is most frequently the friction which occurs where the two jurisdictions overlap and the stratagems used to resolve it, but friction is not inevitable as, for example, when the head of the government takes personal charge of the army in the field and the two jurisdictions merge, or when the war aims are achieved in a few months without much in the way of collateral damage to the economy or to the civilian population. However, the many occasions on which friction does occur suggests very strongly that it is more than a coincidence. Moreover, its consequences are likely to be dire if unresolved – the downfall of a successful general deemed too big for his boots, a military coup, or the war being lost. Understanding the causes of friction is therefore an important area of investigation, and it has been touched on again and again over the centuries in various contexts ranging from detailed studies of individual campaigns to philosophical works such as Thomas Hobbes's Leviathan. But is friction between generals and politicians in the British Wars worthy of study in its own right? In my opinion yes because of its complexity given the number of fronts, armies, generals and civil jurisdictions involved, but establishing a convincing narrative only becomes possible if the investigation is set within a sound analytical framework.

Historians have created a problem for themselves in devising meaningful statements about the struggle over command and control in the British Wars by fighting shy of conceptualisation, and when it is employed to see it merely in terms of strategy and tactics.

Although the definition of tactics differs slightly from book to book, it is almost exclusively employed to describe the actions of generals when they came within striking distance of the enemy with the imminent prospect of a stand-off, a battle, or a siege. In the mid-seventeenth century this aspect of command and control was seen very largely as ultimately the responsibility of the senior officer in charge. However, if Generals Baillie and Leslie were telling the truth rather than attempting to evade responsibility for what occurred on the battlefield, political intervention at the tactical level was

---

[1] Sir Lawrence Freedman, *Command: The Pattern of Military Operations from Korea to Ukraine* (London: Penguin, 2022); *The Guardian*, Saturday, 17 September 2022.

responsible for the unfortunate deployment of Scottish armies at Kilsyth in 1645 and Dunbar in 1650.[2] There is also a strong possibility that the failure of parliament's generals to exploit the advantage they had gained following the Second Battle of Newbury by disrupting the Royalist armies as they left the scene under the cover of darkness owed something to the civilian members of the English parliament who had two of the four votes at the council of war, and also to Oliver Cromwell's determination not to destroy the King's last major army as it retreated because it was not in his interest as a politician with a radical religious agenda for outright victory to be achieved at that point in time.[3]

I have no reservations about the stock definition of tactics. Strategy, however, is another matter altogether in that the term is frequently used in a very casual manner to cover everything from the hammering out of plans long before the declaration of war to the actual moment when contending armies come face-to-face.[4] The principal weakness in using such a definition for investigating the nature and causes of friction between generals and politicians is that it lumps together three stages in the waging of war: the aims; the discussions as to how these are to be achieved on the ground and the resources required for implementing them; and the ways in which the generals sought to turn theory into practice from the start of the campaigns up to the point when tactics kick in.

An alternative classification is provided by Jacques-Antoine-Hippolyte, Comte de Guibert, a professional soldier of the Ancien Regime, in *L'Essaie General de Tactiques* published in 1770. In *L'Essaie* de Guibert reflected on the success of Frederick the Great's oblique order of attack, but he also looked forward to the art of war as practiced by Napoleon which rejected the static and formulaic and emphasised mobility and imagination in both attack and defence. In his discussion of the art of war he opted for a threefold rather than a two-fold classification – strategy, grand tactics (later often referred to as operations), and tactics, with strategy covering the first two areas mentioned above and operations the third.

That is not to say that the notion of separating strategy from operations is totally missing from writing on the British Civil Wars. Pointing the way is General Sir Frank Kitson's military biography of Cromwell, which should be compulsory reading for all political historians of the British Wars. He clearly showed in his account of the aftermath of the Royalist defeat at Nantwich in January 1644 that it was the King not his senior commanders on the spot who formulated the overall recovery plan based on a new army base at Shrewsbury and then moved resources into the area to make it effective. The upshot was that several weeks later Prince Rupert was able to put together an operation using cavalry and mounted musketeers to relieve the garrison at Newark 50 miles across country, thus saving the vital staging post for communication between Royalist controlled areas in the north and south of England, which was essential to Charles's revised strategic plan for safeguarding the northern Royalists from being squeezed in a pincer movement involving the Scottish army and the English parliament's Eastern Association army.[5]

Gardiner, who is to be admired for consulting with serving or retired soldiers before writing his battle narratives, appeared to teeter on the edge of using de Guibert's classification when he referred

---

2   D. Stevenson, *Revolution and Counter Revolution 1644–51* (Edinburgh: John Donald, 2002), pp.28–29; *A Collection of State Papers of John Thurloe*, T. Birch (ed.), 7 vols. (London: 1742) I. pp.167–68.
3   For the most detailed accounts of this hypothesis see *Warrior Generals: Winning the British Wars* (London: Yale University Press, 2010), pp.129, 135–36 and 'Oliver Cromwell and the Performance of Parliament's Armies in the Newbury Campaign', *History* 96 (2011), pp.9–10.
4   For the messy picture, see Sir Lawrence Freedman, *A History of Strategy* 2nd ed. (Oxford: the University press, 2015).
5   *Old Ironside* (London: Weidenfeld and Nicolson, 2004), pp.72, 74–5.

to the movement of armies in the summer of 1643 as strategic operations, but this did not prevent him kicking over the traces and allowing his imagination to run riot in the field of strategy as defined by de Guibert by conjuring up a three-pronged advance on London by the King's forces in the north, the south-west and the Thames Valley which has no foundation whatsoever in the surviving primary sources.[6]

As for myself, I have clearly been groping towards De Guibert's categorisation for some years beginning with the occasional use of the term operation to describe the follow-up to strategic planning when writing brief descriptions of campaigns.[7] Nevertheless, despite my interest in the nature of generalship, the idea of using his model as a tool for identifying and then assessing the causes of the friction between generals and their political masters only entered my head during recent research into the fighting in Scotland and Ireland.[8] In the interests of brevity, however, I will confine myself primarily to the relationships between the governments at Westminster and their senior commander from the appointment of the earl of Essex as captain general in July 1642 to the destruction of the last Royalist army by Oliver Cromwell at the battle of Worcester in September 1651.

Parliament and its Generals 1642-46

Friction between generals and politicians about their respective roles may have begun before the start of the First Civil War. Gardiner claimed that the earl of Essex, Captain General of parliament's army, was resentful at its refusal to accept his request that he should be appointed lord high constable of England with full powers to negotiate with the King, but the evidence for it is circumstantial in the extreme, namely the report of a Frenchman observing events in this country in the light of his knowledge of French history.[9] A more likely cause was the wording of Essex's commission issued in late July 1642. This appeared to give him supreme authority over all the forces raised by parliament, but it was to be exercised 'according to such instructions as he should receive from time to time from both Houses of Parliament'.[10] Clearly this could affect matters operational and even tactical, but it is unlikely to have explained the foul temper the earl displayed when he left London six weeks later to take charge of parliament's field army which was coming together at Northampton in response to the King's raising of the royal standard at Nottingham. Nevertheless the earl was soon to experience the effect of the first of such instructions on his conduct of the war.

By late September the King had moved from Nottingham to Shrewsbury with Essex responding by taking up quarters at Worcester to prevent the Royalist army moving farther down the Severn valley into potential recruiting areas like Herefordshire and south-east Wales where he had much support from local landowners. The move westwards rather than in the direction of London reduced

---

6   S.R. Gardiner, *History of the Great Civil War 1642–1649*, 4 vols. (London: Longmans, 1888–91) I, p.231. I first discovered Gardiner's error when writing about the war in the area to the south of the Thames in my BA dissertation, and in my MA thesis an alternative strategy was proposed. A more tightly argued version appeared in print in *Southern History* 3 (1981), pp.55–79. This was subsequently expanded to include the strategy intended for Marquis of Newcastle's northern army to execute. It was published in M. Wanklyn and F. Jones, *A Military History of the English Civil War* (Harlow: Pearson/Longman, 2005), pp.92–94, 126–27.
7   M. Wanklyn, *Decisive Battles of the English Civil Wars: Myth and Reality* (Barnsley: Pen and Sword, 2006), pp. 136, 162.
8   Wanklyn and Jones, *A Military History*; M. Wanklyn, *The Army of Occupation in Ireland* (Solihull: Helion and co., 2022).
9   Gardiner, *Great Civil War*, I, p.20; M. Wanklyn, *Parliament's Generals* (Barnsley: Pen and Sword, 2019), p.8.
10 C.H. Firth and R.S. Rait, *Acts and Ordinances of the Interregnum* 3 vols. (London: HMSO 1911) I, pp.14–16.

the likelihood of a battle, and it also raised the possibility that Charles was finding such difficulty in raising sufficient men to form an army that he might well seize the chance of giving up his resort to arms if the right noises came from Westminster. Initially Essex had been empowered to seize the person of the King by force if necessary even if this involved a battle, but now he was instructed not to make a hostile move until Charles had had the chance to reply to a petition from parliament that he was to deliver via a personal emissary.[11] Whether or not this procedure met with his approval is not known. If not he would have been disappointed if not angry at not being able to display his war winning capabilities.

When the Royalists seemed on the verge of leaving Shrewsbury with London as their likely destination parliament issued new instructions. Essex was to shadow the King's army and engage it in battle if he felt that he had a clear advantage.[12] But for the moment the lord general did not stir as its first day's march was down the Severn valley towards Worcester, but when on 13 October it suddenly moved off in the direction of Birmingham and Charles refused three days later to accept what he described as a petition from traitors, he prepared to intercept it. This he did in south Warwickshire on the 23rd. Despite Essex's earlier claim that his army was ready to leave Worcester whenever this became militarily necessary, he clearly fought the battle of Edgehill at a disadvantage. The King had his entire army with him, whereas some of the lord general's regiments were too far away to join him whilst others were a day's march behind escorting the siege train.[13] This lack of readiness was the first sign of Parliament's disquiet about its general's enthusiasm for the war especially as he had responded to the rejection of the petition with the words 'I expected no better'.

It may not, however, have been entirely his decision not to draw in his infantry quartered at Gloucester and Hereford and his troops of cavalry guarding crossings of the river Avon at Evesham and probably elsewhere. He was probably under what was at the very least an informal restraint on his ability to make decisions without external intervention. Soon after reaching Worcester, parliament sent him an order that he was to pay attention to a so-called committee of assistance made up of the MPs and peers holding commissions in his army, which was to discuss matters he considered important. Admittedly it was up to him to convene the committee with nothing being said about his having to accept the advice it offered, but reports on their resolutions were to be sent to parliament and he would have found it difficult to ignore a firm recommendation supported by a majority of the members given the wording of his commission.[14] However, it is impossible to ascertain the effect that meetings of the informal committee had on the first moves in the 1642 campaign. Occasionally its reports were mentioned in the journals of the Two Houses, but its contact would have been with the Committee of Safety set up by parliament to manage the war, whose minutes and ingoing and outgoing correspondence no longer survive.[15]

Indirect evidence of political interference in decision-making but at the tactical level does, however, exist for what was the last day of the campaign when the two armies were facing each other at Turnham Green five miles to the west of London. After the severe mauling of one of Essex's regiments at Brentford on 12 November the Royalists had advanced too far for their own good and faced the prospect of being surrounded. They were also heavily outnumbered, but their only means of escape was

---

11 Rushworth, *Historical Collections of Private Passages of State* 8 vols. (London: J. Browne reprint, 1721) V, p.16; Wanklyn, *Warrior Generals*, pp.17–18.
12 Journal of the House of Lords (JHL) V, pp.402–03 (15 October 1642).
13 Wanklyn and Jones, *A Military History*, pp. 45–47; Wanklyn, *Warrior Generals*, pp.22–23.
14 JHL V, pp.369–70; journal of the House of Commons (JHC), II, pp.769–70, 775.
15 For its reports sent to the Two Houses see, for example, JHC II, p.806, JHL V, p.423.

across a bridge over the river Brent at Brentford. Seeing the chance of cutting off their retreat Essex ordered several of his regiments to bypass the Royalist position to the north via Acton and seize the bridge, but the march was abandoned on his orders when it was well under way and the King's army were allowed to disengage unscathed.

Gardiner blamed the earl's military advisers who, having gained their experience in the static fighting in the Netherlands, were adverse to such a bold move, but this does not seem to have been the case. Sir John Merrick, who carried the command to cancel it to the officers in charge of the flanking movement, was such a man, but he was so angry about it that he used intemperate words about those who had put pressure on Essex to do so. The most likely person to have persuaded him that it was the safest course for the whole army to be drawn up on the London side of at Turnham Green was the earl of Holland, a member of the Committee of Safety whose career had been that of a courtier with a dismal record as a senior commander in the First Bishops' War. Edmund Ludlow, who was no friend of the earl of Essex, pointed the finger at Holland in his memoirs, and Holland was praised after the event for his help in deploying parliament's forces confronting the King on 12 November.[16]

During the course of 1643 friction between central government and the earl of Essex is a little easier to discern. The Committee of Safety's strategy for the campaigning season was to encourage its supporters in the provinces to hamstring Royalist recruiting operations there. They were also to cut the routes along which the King would receive military supplies so as to cause problems for the army base he had established at Oxford after Turnham Green which was seen as too close to London for comfort. The first step was for Essex to capture Reading garrisoned during the winter by a brigade of Royalist infantry after which his army was to advance on Oxford and force the King to fight or flee. Essex duly set about preparing to set siege to Reading and to that end ordered Lord Grey of Wark and Sir William Waller, the commanders of two of the new armies which were being raised in East Anglia and in the south and west of England respectively, to join him. The first obeyed; the second did not. Sir William, who had attracted the attention of influential members of the House of Commons as a possible replacement for Essex following a succession of minor victories against the King's supporters in the south of England from Chichester to the Forest of Dean during the winter and early spring, moved in the opposite direction and captured the city of Hereford instead but without having the manpower to hold it. Nevertheless, Essex managed to force the Reading garrison to surrender after seeing off the King's army which had tried to relieve the town. If he complained about Waller's behaviour as challenging his ability to run the war as he wished it fell on deaf ears probably because it had not affected the outcome of the siege.

The lord general's next move should have been to advance through the Goring gap into the middle Thames valley. Various factors of a military nature both direct and indirect were given subsequently to explain why it had not happened: shortage of pay for the parliament's troops; limited supplies of equipment; the army's weakness in cavalry; disease spreading through the ranks; and most insistently the Lord General's lethargy compared with Waller, which now increasingly was being seen as a lack of commitment to outright victory. One thing however can be said with a fair degree of certainty: if Essex had made a determined move towards Oxford, the King would have left for the north of England with such troops as he could mount despite a fortified camp being hurriedly constructed in a bend in the river Thames near Abingdon defending the approaches to the city. This it now seems was no more than a bluff. Firepower was essential for a fortified camp to withstand an attack and the King's arsenal in New College had very little gunpowder left.

---

16 Edmund Ludlow, *Memoirs*, C.H. Firth ed. 2 vols. (Oxford: the University Press, 1894) I, p.47; JHL V, p.17.

However, the principal reason for the Thames Valley operation grinding to a halt after the capture of Reading was political rather than military. Peace talks at Oxford had stalled in March, but some members of the Committee of Safety were in contact with the Queen in the hope that she could persuade her husband to enter into a further round of negotiations, and as a mark of good faith she demanded a temporary ceasefire in the Thames Valley. This met with the approval of members of the Committee of Safety in the know and fighting ceased, though in the event they had been duped. She had recently arrived at Bridlington in Yorkshire in a ship containing hundreds of barrels of gunpowder purchased in the Netherlands, and her sole aim in talking to the Committee's representative was to win time for a convoy carrying arms and ammunition to pass from York to Oxford and thus enable the King to cling onto his headquarters. Running the gauntlet of provincial forces in the East Midlands that were not affected by the truce, the convoy duly arrived in Oxford on 11 May.[17]

Essex had respected the ceasefire but whether with conviction or resignation is not known, but the negotiations having failed he was expected to get his troops moving again, but by then disease had swept through both the armies at Reading forcing Lord Grey's to return to East Anglia and Essex's to lose much of its capacity to fight. In June he did move into Buckinghamshire beyond the Chilterns in the hope that new quarters would cause illness amongst his troops to abate, but apart from a brief probing of the outer defences of Oxford stalemate ensued during which his army mouldered away despite a succession of increasingly desperate letters to his political masters which seem to have caused a measure of irritation that he had been profligate in the past and was exaggerating his needs. He was also experiencing trouble from Sir William Waller who once again had showed no respect for his orders but knew he could do so without reprisal because of the support he enjoyed in the House of Commons.

The Lord General's inability to control the operations of other generals came to a head in late May when a brigade left Oxford under the command of the Marquis of Hertford seeking recruits in Wiltshire and Somerset. Essex ordered Waller to do something about it as the counties fell within his jurisdiction as major general of a chain of counties from Worcestershire to Somerset, but instead he marched off in the opposite direction intent on capturing Worcester leaving a negligible military presence in the southern counties for which he was responsible. The operation failed and as Essex had foreseen the consequences were dire for parliament's retaining control over south-central England as the Royalists had used the fortnight's grace to create a formidable army in west Somerset from troops raised locally supported by regiments raised in Devon and Cornwall.[18]

Waller could not have moved on Worcester without the connivance of the Committee of Safety dazzled by his earlier victories, but when his army was destroyed at Roundway Down on 13 July followed a fortnight later by the Royalists storming Bristol whose garrison was too weak to defend it Waller having withdrawn hundreds of men to fight the Royalist army of the west. Common sense then prevailed. After these immense blows to its conduct of the war parliament agreed to recruit and adequately resource Essex's army, and to support it with a brigade of the London trained bands after having consult him about how best to recover the strategic initiative. There were three possible ways Essex's army could help – the successful relief of Gloucester or Exeter currently besieged by the King's troops or a direct attack on Oxford. In the event the Committee of Safety accepted the lord general's advice to focus exclusively on Gloucester, which was much nearer than Exeter and more likely to be successful than setting siege to Oxford. He was to command the expedition whilst Waller was to raise a new army in the London area charged with the defence of the capital and the counties of Kent, Surrey,

---

17　Wanklyn and Jones, *A Military History*, pp.88–89; Wanklyn, *Parliament's Generals*, pp.16–17.
18　Wanklyn and Jones, *A Military History*, pp.87–88; Wanklyn, *Warring Generals* pp.2–6, 53–54.

Sussex and Hampshire. For the moment friction between the lord general and the MPs had therefore eased. They could only stem the Royalist tide by working together and paying no attention to the talk of Waller's wife and friends that Sir William had lost at Roundway Down because Essex failed to respond to his requests for assistance.[19]

Having successfully relieved Gloucester in August and fought the King's army to a standstill at Newbury on 20 September 1643 without the help of Waller whose new army was taking a time to raise, Essex managed to increase his authority over Sir William as a reward for his successes,[20] but he then made a fundamental mistake by refusing to stir himself into challenging Prince Rupert's efforts to establish a Royalist presence in Northamptonshire and Bedfordshire which threatened parliament's control over East Anglia thus causing charges of lethargy and lack of commitment to outright victory to re-emerge with redoubled force.

The comeback came in the first three months of 1644. Parliament was extremely slow in providing the money to fit out his army for the coming campaigning season. In addition his control over operations was severely curtailed in several respects. An alliance between parliament and the Scottish government concluded in August 1643 meant that the war against the King became a joint effort in which some concessions had to be made to Scottish military conventions which included the politicians having a stricter control over the army commanders. At the same time Essex's powers over armies other than his own were much reduced. A revitalised army of the Eastern Association, now under the command of the Earl of Manchester, was freed from the Captain General's control and his right to give orders to Waller's army would only apply if parliament ordered the two armies to conduct a joint operation.

In February 1644 the Committee of Both Kingdoms which, as its title indicated, included several Scottish members, was established and it quickly agreed on the strategy that was to inform the first two months' campaigns in the south of England. Essex and Manchester's armies were to remain in the counties to the north and west of London keeping in check the King's field army operating out of Oxford whilst Waller reconquered the counties of the south west he had lost in 1643. This it followed up with a flurry of operational commands, which began with Essex being ordered to send his cavalry regiments to help Waller when Sir Ralph Hopton, the Royalist general he was facing in Hampshire, was understood to be about to receive reinforcements from Oxford.[21]

This new yoke was loathed by all three army commanders. Essex and his supporters tried twice to have it abolished, and during the course of the year each in turn showed that he thought he knew better how the war should be run by disregarding the orders issued by the English politicians on the committee and their Scottish friends. The first was Sir William Waller. Having soundly defeated Hopton at the battle of Cheriton on 29 March, he refused to lead his army beyond the borders of Hampshire because of the size of the army the King had assembled on his flank near Hungerford in west Berkshire. By 17 April to the Committee of Both Kingdom's annoyance he and his army were back at Farnham, the base from which they had set out on the Cheriton campaign.[22]

Six weeks later Essex and Waller, having advanced on Oxford from Reading and forced the King to leave his headquarters for the Severn valley with a flying army of cavalry and mounted musketeers, disobeyed the Committee's strategic instructions that Essex should pursue the King whilst Waller

---

19   Wanklyn and Jones, *A Military History*, pp.103–05, 114–15. For a discussion of the arguments surrounding the charge against Essex, see *Warring Generals*, pp.106–07.
20   J. Adair, *Roundhead General: the Campaigns of Sir William Waller* 2nd ed. (Stroud: Sutton Publishing, 1997), pp.120–24.
21   Wanklyn, *Decisive Battles*, pp.83–84.
22   Wanklyn and Jones, *A Military History*, pp.146–48.

overran the west of England on the sound military grounds that the Captain General's army with its slow moving train of artillery and high ratio of infantry to cavalry would be incapable of keeping tabs on the King's highly mobile force whilst Waller with his numerous cavalry and dragoons clearly could. The Earl therefore set out for Dorset and Devon whilst Sir William remained in the West Midlands dedicated to preventing the King from returning to Oxford and resurrecting his field army or riding north to assist Prince Rupert's operations in Lancashire. Parliament and the Committee of Both Kingdoms were incensed, but Essex had advanced too far into the west of England for them to stop him and they grudgingly let the matter drop when Weymouth, Barnstaple and Taunton fell into his hands and his troops overran the south-west as far as the river Tamar.

The Earl of Manchester took longer to disobey the Committee's orders. Released in early May from operations in the Oxford area his army had performed magnificently at the battle of Marston Moor against Prince Rupert fought in cooperation with the Scottish army and parliament's army of the north on 2 July. The Committee of Both Kingdoms then accepted the advice of the three commanders-in-chief that their forces should go their separate ways to fully exploit their victory with the Scots capturing the remaining Royalist garrisons in the far north, the northern army focusing on those in the north and east ridings of Yorkshire, and the Eastern Association army on those in Sheffield and the adjacent areas of Derbyshire and Lincolnshire. The only additional instruction was that Manchester's army should also keep a close eye on the defeated Royalists who had escaped across the Pennines and to take steps to disperse them if they seemed to be regrouping.[23] However, when the Eastern Association army had largely completed its quota of siege operations, there was alarm at Westminster at what turned out to be faulty intelligence of the success of that Rupert's recruiting operations, and the Committee ordered it to advance on Chester, the Prince's headquarters, rather than to set siege to Newark as local Parliamentarians wanted. The cavalry officers disliked the idea of the march on Chester and persuaded Manchester to argue their case. The Committee, however, was adamant, but before the operation was properly underway it was overtaken by events: the Earl of Essex's army had been decisively defeated in Cornwall and its infantry regiments forced to surrender on Lostwithiel.[24]

Manchester's army was then given a very different strategic objective, namely to help repair the damage to parliament's war effort in the south by moving as quickly as possible from its base at Lincoln to a rendezvous with Waller's army and Essex's cavalry in Dorset. Manchester demurred and as a result it was six weeks before the Committee had gathered together a force capable of winning a victory over the King's forces. It was incontrovertible that Manchester had been dragging his feet, and at the time and since it was alleged that he wished to avoid a battle because it would end the chance of the war ending by negotiation. However, I have argued forcibly that Manchester's motives were not political but military and based on very sound operational thinking. It was essential for the army group confronting the King's forces as they emerged from the west country to be large enough to be confident of victory, and this would only be so if it included a brigade of the London trained bands and the Earl of Essex's infantry regiments which were recruiting in Portsmouth and the Isle of Wight neither of which could not be expected to arrive at a rendezvous before the second half of October. If the Eastern Association army in conjunction with Waller's and Essex's exhausted cavalry had faced the King's forces in Dorset three weeks earlier as had been the Committee's intention it would have been outnumbered and facing

---

23 CSPD 1644, pp.385–86, 406.
24 Wanklyn, *Warrior Generals*, pp.125–26.

almost certain defeat leaving no force at parliament's command in the south or the midlands capable of blocking the King's advance on London.[25]

The reaction of the politicians to yet another questioning of their control of the war was to send two members of the Committee of Both Kingdoms to the rendezvous of the three armies and the associated brigade, which took place at Basingstoke on 20/21 October. The ostensible reason was to prevent quarrels between the generals causing operational paralysis and possibly a catastrophe on the battlefield, but their remit was clearly a reflection of Scottish practice that soldiers alone could not be trusted as the last battle of the Civil War was clearly in prospect.[26] As members of a tiny council of war chosen by the Committee to manage the campaign they would have the authority to steer decision-making in such a way as to ensure that its instructions were obeyed, and a practicable tactical plan devised. If they failed or had any doubts about the decision they could call on it to adjudicate as the fighting would be taking place within 30 miles of Westminster.

The effect of the 10 days' presence of the two civilian representatives on the army group's council of war is impossible to discern behind the smokescreen of bland comments contained in their correspondence with the Committee the principal theme of which was that the generals were doing as well as could be expected given the time of year, but it could not be denied that the tactics employed by the council of war on the battlefield at Newbury on 27 October not achieved their objective of surrounding the enemy forces and causing them to surrender, and that when informed that they were escaping in the early evening moonlight they took no action whatsoever to impede them.[27] However, during the fortnight of the campaigning season that remained after their return to London, they were not subject to hostile questioning as the generals covered their backs by failing to carry out any of the instructions sent them by the Committee blaming the weather and the sheer exhaustion of their troops. The Newbury campaign thus ended in stalemate with none of the Committee's strategic objectives for the second half of 1644 achieved. Its generals had not succeeded in conjuring up about a second Marston Moor in the south of England; the territory lost in the summer of 1643 was still largely in Royalist hands; and Oxford remained the King's headquarters defended by his field army its morale much improved by the campaigns it had just fought.

During the winter, parliament undertook a thorough-scale reform of its forces in the south and the midlands designed to remove some of the causes of friction between the generals and the politicians and consolidate its control over the conduct of the war. The complexity of command was reduced by creating the New Model Army from the best units in the armies of Essex, Manchester and Waller with the three generals losing their commands. As the new commander in chief it appointed Sir Thomas Fairfax, the deputy commander of its army in the north, who was known to be an enterprising commander in attack and defence, totally committed to winning the war, of an obedient temperament and without a conspicuous record of wanting to run the war in his own way. Nevertheless, as a precaution the wording of his commission placed him firmly in a subordinate position to the Committee of Both Kingdoms.

---

25 M. Wanklyn, 'A General Much Maligned', *War in History* 14 (2007), pp.144–45.
26 CSPD 1644–45, pp.39–40.
27 At the time only four of the eight men named were present and allowed to vote, namely the two civilians, Sir William Waller and Oliver Cromwell. Essex was ill; his deputy Lord Robartes still in London; Waller's deputy Haselrig excluded from voting on a technicality; and the Earl of Manchester on the opposite side of the battlefield with the Royalist army in between: Wanklyn, Oliver Cromwell and the Newbury Campaign, pp.9–10, 15–16.

However, vesting so much authority in the hands of the politicians did not remove all the causes of friction insofar as the General was concerned. Fairfax faced exactly the same problems as Essex had faced in 1642 and 1643 – political interference with operations and having to take the blame when they did not meet expectations, but he also had to endure a barrage of letters from the Committee of Both Kingdoms designed to micromanage his campaigns the first of which was to obey its strategic instructions to relieve the besiege garrison at Taunton in Somerset, one of the few permanent gains of Essex's campaign in the west country, which was rightly believed to be on the verge of being stormed.

Having reached central Dorset, however, he was ordered to return to the Thames Valley in order to set siege to Oxford the King having seized the opportunity to leave his headquarters through a hole created in the blockade at a distance around the Royalist headquarters overseen by Oliver Cromwell. Sir Thomas duly weakened his army by four regiments, which continued towards Taunton and succeeded in relieving the garrison, but when they tried to return they found their way was blocked by a much larger Royalist force. There was no alternative to returning to Taunton where they remained in straitened circumstances until they were rescued by the rest of the army in early July.

Fairfax had not wanted to downscale the operation to relieve Taunton and was far from content that the only reason he had been recalled to the Thames Valley was that members of the Committee had been led astray by their ambition to end the war as quickly as possible by the most successful royalist intelligence coup of the war, namely the suggestion that senior officers in the Oxford garrison were prepared to surrender it when provided with the excuse that they were about to be overwhelmed by a superior force. Whilst the farce of a siege went on without Fairfax having the resources to make dents in the by now formidable defences around the city, the King's army had surged through the midlands causing the besiegers of the city of Chester to flee for safety across the river Mersey when it was still 20 miles to the south, and then storming Leicester, which raised the prospect that it would follow this up by either invading the Eastern Association or marching north to attack the Scottish army.

Like Essex before him Fairfax was initially blamed for his inactivity, and when he did abandon the siege on the Committee's orders and march north to confront the King's army, he made the mistake of trying to win favour by capturing one of Oxford's out-garrisons rather than marching hell for leather for East Anglia. What followed were charges that he was clearly too inexperienced to be in high command on his own, and that members of the Committee should join his council of war and lead him by the hand in the enemy's direction.

The provision of 'politicians' to chivvy Sir Thomas into being operationally pro-active was first raised by the city of London immediately after the fall of Leicester. The proposal led to three days of serious discussion in the Committee of Both Kingdoms in the second week of June 1645, but in the end the Committee decided not to implement it. Instead it declared that it did not have sufficient members to spare to form a sub-committee in the army, and merely ordered Fairfax, having consulted his council of war, to pursue the King's army wherever it went and to destroy it in battle, which meant operational and tactical independence. Gardiner claimed that military questions were now at last to be answered by military men, but this is an exaggeration.[28] Fairfax's activities were still subject to a measure of control either through orders from parliament directed to him personally or through letters sent by the Committee on parliament's instructions.

The new commander-in-chief followed up his victory at Naseby on 16 June with the recapture of Leicester, but then what? Given the scale of the victory a strategic decision was necessary. Should the New Model pursue the King and his surviving cavalry into South Wales where he would be busy

---

28   *History of the Great Civil War* II, pp.211, 237–38.

recruiting new infantry regiments to replace the ones lost at Naseby, or should it head for Taunton, rescue the corps that had missed Naseby, and inflict a similarly decisive defeat on the 10,000 Royalist troops under the command of General George Goring besieging the town? It was a strategic decision Fairfax did not feel empowered to take on his own, and for several days he took his army on a route to the south that made it possible for him to lead it subsequently either in a south westerly direction or due west depending on the orders he received from Westminster. When they arrived they were for him to head for Taunton, his preferred option, to which was added a reminder that he and his council not the committee were now in control of operations.[29]

In the autumn having given a great fright to Goring's army at Langport, established a chain of garrisons across the narrowest part of the southwestern peninsular to prevent him joining the King, and capturing Bristol by storm, Fairfax prepared to move against the Royalist general's demoralised troops in Devon and Cornwall, but parliament thought otherwise. Under pressure from MPs representing counties and boroughs in south-central England it instructed him to detach a corps under Oliver Cromwell's command to reduce the remaining important Royalist garrisons still holding out in that area, first Devizes, then Winchester and finally Basing House. The operation was a conspicuous success, but it took six weeks to complete and caused a delay in the operation to drive the Royalists from Devon and Cornwall before winter set int, though the advance did begin just before Cromwell and his regiments returned. But even after the operation began Fairfax did not have complete control over his army. Fears that serious raiding would disrupt the economy of the home counties and London's food supplies came to the surface at Westminster when the King returned to his headquarters for the winter with 2,000 cavalry after making a foray into parts of Huntingdonshire that had not previously experienced any fighting on the last leg of his journey. The commander-in-chief was therefore ordered to weaken his force by sending several cavalry regiments back east to serve as a deterrent despite the fact that the Royalists still holding out in the far west had 3,000 horse at their disposal, but as with the operations against the enemy at Taunton in May and around Oxford in early June Fairfax grumbled but obeyed.[30]

The struggle between generals and politicians over the conduct of war had thus been seemingly resolved by the end of the First Civil War with strategy and the control of resources remaining under political control but the conduct of operations very largely left to Fairfax advised by his council of war.

The First Army Coup and its Consequences

The victory over the King's forces in England brought with it the collapse of the winning coalition as differences between the war aims of what were described at the time as the Peace and the War Party. The classification is in my opinion problematic, but it was extensively used at the time when it was believed that one element amongst the Parliamentarians favoured the war ending by negotiation and the other by outright victory. However, the terms offered to the King on various occasions during the war by Peace Party representatives and the reception given to his counter proposals were so unyielding that they could not have expected an agreement to be reached. The first one of which had wanted the war to end by negotiation and the second for parliament to win an outright victory before talking to the King, though the Peace Party is a bit of a misnomer as the terms they had on offer did not fall far short

---

29 Wanklyn and Jones, *Military History*, p.255.
30 M. Wanklyn, *Parliament's Generals: Supreme Command and Politics in the British Wars* (Barnsley: Pen and Sword, 2019), pp.101–07.

of complete capitulation on Charles's part. Moreover, the bitter rivalry, which had been kept in check by the need for solidarity against a formidable Royalist enemy, was exacerbated by the politicisation of the New Model Army, which was itself similarly divided.[31]

The downward spiral from triumph to near civil war, which took less than a year, has been intensively explored and debated from Gardiner's time onwards. It falls outside the parameters of this study of command and control, but what has often been lost in the process is the undeniable fact that it was dislike of the strategy for reasserting English hegemony in Ireland devised by the 'Peace Party' that led to a head-to-head confrontation between parliament and the army in mid-March 1647 which within a few weeks can no longer be described as friction but rather as conflagration.

Putting down the rebellion against the English hegemony in Ireland which had begun in October 1641 had been put on hold at the outbreak of the First English Civil War, but it began to attract some attention immediately after the blows administered by the New Model Army to the King's field armies at Naseby and Langport. For a year, however, there was little progress. The military situation in Ireland gave no major cause for concern, whilst in England the war was still going at full pelt in the midlands and south-west of the country. This ensured that it enjoy primacy in parliament's allocation of military resources with some assigned to Ireland being diverted elsewhere before they were shipped.[32] There were also profound delays in sending reinforcements. Regiments composed of volunteers and impressed men, in the case of Colonel Sterling's infantry regiment, or existing formations not in parliament's field armies such as Colonel Jephson's Hampshire horse, did not leave for many months after being approved by the English parliament's Irish committee.[33] Unsurprisingly the trickle that did reach Ireland in 1645 and early 1646 sometimes arrived too late as was the case with Duncannon fort guarding the approaches to Waterford harbour, which had held out against patriot forces since December 1641 despite Waterford having been in patriot hands the entire time.[34]

Following the surrender of the King's last remaining major garrisons in June and July 1646 parliament issued orders for additional troops to be sent to Ireland drawn from provincial units which were being disbanded, but progress was still slow. In the interests of speeding it up the Peace Party in the House of Commons proposed on 31 July that four regiments of foot and two of horse from the New Model Army should be sent there immediately. An opportunist follow-up to the large majority achieved in a vote taken earlier in the day, the motion was lost by a single vote probably because uncommitted MPs voted with the War Party convinced by the case for sending a third of the New Model's infantry to Ireland being too risky. England's security was threatened by a French and/ or Scottish invasion on the King's behalf and by unrest in parliament's provincial forces being disbanded due to grievances concerning pay arrears and fears that soldiers would be prosecuted for civil and criminal offences committed during the war.[35]

Momentum increased during the autumn and the winter. More and more regiments were commissioned; the principal reason being a major deterioration in the military situation that meant that assistance was needed immediately as the Irish patriots were threatening to overrun the whole of the

---

31 M. Wanklyn, *Parliament's Generals* (Barnsley: Pen and Sword, 2019), p.39.
32 JHL, VII, p.519.
33 CSPI 1633–47, pp.408–17, 431, 451, 454, 481–82, 486, 491, 495–96.
34 JHL, VIII, p.496. For the investigation of the surrender and off the inadequate support from parliament's navy see the witnesses' statements in Sir John Gilbert, *History of the Irish Confederation and the War in Ireland* 7 vols. (Dublin, 1882–91) IV, pp.210–38.
35 JHC IV, pp,631–32. For the fullest account of this episode, see J.R. MacCormack, *Revolutionary Politics in the Long Parliament* (Cambridge, Massachusetts: Harvard University Press, 1973), pp.130–31.

country. The Protestant army in Ulster had been badly mauled at the battle of Benburb in June, whilst the Marquis of Ormond commanding the Royalist forces in the Dublin area was in danger of being overwhelmed. This was due to the patriots and parliament having disowned the cessation the Marquis had negotiated on the King's behalf in 1643, which had enabled him to send most of his troops to England to support the King's cause but severely weakened his ability to respond to the new threat.[36]

The Peace party announced its strategy for progressing the Protestant cause in Ireland on 28 January 1647. This was for a vigorous offensive war to be carried out by an army large enough it implied to reconquer those parts of the country controlled by the patriots. The Two Houses estimated five weeks later that for the strategy to succeed the New Model Army must provide seven regiments of foot and two (later four) of horse. Following Ormond's willingness to hand over his garrisons to parliament in return for a safe passage to Europe, two New Model regiments of foot were to be sent to Ireland immediately to strengthen the garrisons at Dublin and Drogheda. The five New Model regiments of foot not to leave England were to be disbanded, leaving the country's security to be defended by eight New Model regiments of horse supplemented by what was left of the provincial infantry garrisoning the principal towns and castles.[37]

Initially there was little doubt that it was the belief in parliament that immediately on receiving the order to march the New Model army units identified for service in Ireland would up sticks and head for the ports. However, it soon became apparent that this was not to be. Instead the officers made demands of parliament that must be accepted before they would agree to leave the country. Some were material in nature concerning such matters as pay arrears and indemnity from prosecution for offences committed during the war, but two related directly or indirectly to Ireland: which regiments were to be sent there and who was to command them given that one provision in the slimming down of the New Model was that members of the Two Houses should no longer hold commands in the army.

Matters came to a head at meetings between army officers with representatives of the two Houses at Saffron Walden between 20 and 22 March,[38] but the writing had been on the wall for a few weeks. On 16 February Sir Thomas Fairfax in a letter to his father wrote that such had been the criticism of the army that 'the soldiery will more willingly lay down their arms than engage themselves in any other service unless they like the conditions they go upon'. After the meetings at Saffron Walden he commented that 'it may seem strange the army doth make propositions to Parliament about going to Ireland', but that it was better than allowing resentment to build up to such a point that mutiny broke out.[39]

Rumours were also circulating in the press that regiments such as Colonel Rich's would refuse to leave England, but parliament would also have had advance warning of what it was up against from the letter it had received from Colonel Hammond, who was to command the New Model regiments to be sent overseas immediately, reported to the Commons on 12 March in which he laid down stringent conditions that must be dealt with before he would leave for Ireland. He demanded a clear statement as to how many troops he would be commanding who were already in Ireland and made stipulations regarding pay and victualling. He must also be appointed as governor of Dublin *pro temp*; his regiment

---

36　JHL, VIII, pp.378–79; J. Scott Wheeler, *The Irish and British Wars 1637–1654* (London: Routledge, 2022), pp.88–89, 172–74.
37　JHC, V, pp.68, 107, 109; CSPD 1645–47, pp.525, 531, 534. The intervening period had been taken up with debates and decisions about the size and composition of the force to remain in England.
38　JHL, IX, pp.112–13.
39　Robert Bell, *Memorials of the Civil War comprising the Correspondence of the Fairfax Family* 2 vols. (London: R. Bentley, 1849) I, pp.332–34.

was to be absent from England for no longer than three months; and he was to have the authority to commandeer shipping if a week before the secondment expired nothing suitable had arrived in port to carry his troops home. The House of Commons' response was to make encouraging noises but then to pass the matter over to a committee for its advice on how to proceed.[40]

The fact that parliament knew that an issue bigger than pay arrears and material conditions was at stake is apparent in the wording of the so-called Declaration of Dislike passed by both Houses on 31 March in response to the circulation of petitions within the army involving all ranks in which some officers were taking the lead one of whom was Colonel Hammond. The very idea that part of the army was questioning parliament's supremacy in military matters was regarded as outrageous. Charles I had recognised this as the fundamental element of monarchical sovereignty in 1642 and cited it as a reason for not giving his assent to a piece of legislation that would have forced him to do so, and parliament's resolve to keep control of strategy is summed up in the condemnation of the petitioners for claiming the right: 'to put conditions on parliament and obstruct the relief of Ireland'.[41]

After that both parties stepped back and negotiations ensued for two months, during which parliament made concession after concession designed to allay concern about the army's material grievances. However, early on it was clear that whole regiments were no longer fit or willing to serve in Ireland, that new ones would have to be raised from scratch from New Model Army volunteers, and that to facilitate the process all the foot regiments would be disbanded, but when the two Houses' representatives tried to put this into effect on 1 June 1647 the response was mutiny. The leaders of the Peace Party in the Commons tried to fight back by political means during June and July, with the New Model volunteers ordered to the Bristol area under their new officers for embarkation. When, however, its supporters in London took to the streets and invaded the parliament building claiming that the MPs and peers had been wrong to rely on appeasement to stem trouble in the army, it provided the justification for its marching into the capital and carrying out a virtually bloodless coup.[42]

As a result the army became to all intents and purposes sovereign with the ability to bend parliament to its will by the threat of force and with the whip hand over both strategy and operations. Needless to say the Peace Party strategy for using the New Model to subdue Ireland passed from the scene with reinforcements sent there in the second half of 1647 and early 1648 becoming available through the disbandment of the almost all the non-garrison regiments in south and central England that were still in pay but not part of the New Model. The effectiveness of the War Party's strategy was confirmed by victories against the patriots at Dungan's Hill and Knocknanuss during the late summer and autumn of 1647, but exploiting such successes was dependent on a steady supply of men and munitions. This fell to a trickle in March 1648 with the outbreak of a second civil war in England and Wales and the prospect of a Scottish invasion in support of the neo-Royalists.[43]

Parliament's war cabinet, the Derby House Committee, was established in early January 1648 to replace the Committee of Both Kingdom, but with a preponderance of members of the Two Houses with little or no military expertise and with only the Earl of Manchester having the experience of commanding an army. Its minutes and its outgoing correspondence with the Commander in Chief read like a return to 1645 but without the sharpness of language that Fairfax had endured in the autumn and winter of that year, which is not surprising as prominent Peace Party members had not been

---

40 HMC, Duke of Portland Mss I, p.414; JHC v, pp.109, 112; the issue of the *Perfect Diurnal* for 15-22/3/1647 cited in M. Kishlansky, *The Rise of the New Model Army* (Cambridge: The University Press, 1979), p.189.
41 JHL ix, pp.112–15.
42 Wanklyn, *Parliament's Generals*, pp.113–16.
43 Scott Wheeler, *Irish and British Wars*, pp.160–61.

nominated.[44] Tact is clear in the committee's instructions, which frequently desired rather than ordered commanders in the field to take action.[45] Its communications with commanders in the field also often made it clear in the first few words that it was merely acting as parliament's mouthpiece.[46]

It was normal practice for parliament to take the lead in strategic decision-making even if this was not immediately apparent. For example, it welcomed Sir Thomas Fairfax's decision in late March to send forces to Pembrokeshire in response to an uprising of local forces incensed about being disbanded without their officers' and soldiers' arrears and grievances being addressed to their satisfaction. Although this was seemingly a strategic initiative, he had merely been following an order issued by the House of Commons in mid-March which he had not immediately obeyed.[47] On the other hand the politicians left the conduct of military operations to the commanders in the field. When a major insurrection occurred in Kent in late May 1648 which threatened London, Fairfax was informed that neither parliament nor the committee at Derby House would interfere in his running of the campaign.[48] The outcome was the victory at Maidstone on the 31st, followed by the clearing of Kent of insurgents during June. Despite the fact that the hard core of the insurgents escaped across the Thames into Essex and the war in the south dragged on for another 13 weeks there was no attempt by the politicians to interfere with how the general ran the campaign.

Parliament did, however, take an interest in moving units around the country in the interests of security. Sometimes it did this by drawing Fairfax's attention to the problem as in the case of unrest in the counties immediately to the north and west of London in late May 1648 and again in July.[49] On other occasions it was more pro-active as, for instance, when it ordered Fairfax to do something about the defence of Bristol on 1 May for fear that the serious unrest in Pembrokeshire that had threatened to spread throughout south Wales would cross the river Severn, and again on 6 June when on receiving intelligence that the Yorkshire Royalists had seized Pontefract Castle. it ordered the Committee at Derby House and the Commander in Chief to consider what forces could be sent north from Wales or elsewhere to help deal with what was now a major uprising and likely in the near future to be supported by a Scottish army.[50] However, it does not seem to have acted without first listening to Fairfax other than in the crisis situation of early August 1648. Then it ordered the New Model army regiment in garrison at Gloucester and other units, both New Model and non-New Model, stationed elsewhere that need not remain where they were for security reasons, to join the forces gathering in Yorkshire for a confrontation with the Scottish army which had crossed the border into England and after some initial hesitation was about to resume its march.[51]

When differences of opinion concerning the resources to be allotted to the various fronts in the Second Civil War in the interests of security arose, they were resolved in due course by compromise in

---

44 JHC V, p.416.
45 The dictionary definition of desire as a verb is to want something very strongly; M. Wanklyn, 'The political career of Edward, 2nd earl of Manchester 1645-49', *Cromwelliana*, series III vol. 10 (2021), p.100.
46 See, for instance, CSPD 1648–48, p.61 (the Committee at Derby House to Fairfax, 6 May 1648) enclosing the House of Commons order to go north with a brigade to deal with the Royalist threat on the Scottish border.
47 JHC V, pp.506, 521; CSPD 1648–49, pp.41–41; Rushworth, *Historical Collections* VII, pp.1017, 1033, 1103.
48 CSPD 1648–49, p.577. The wording of the letter was very similar to that which its predecessor had used to reassure Fairfax after the battle of Naseby: Wanklyn. *Warrior Generals*, p.167; Wanklyn, *Parliament's Generals*, pp.87–89, 104–05.
49 CSPD 1648-9, p.125; Gardiner, *Great Civil War* IV, pp.159–61.
50 JHC V, pp.549, 587; CSPD 1648–49, p.54, 115.
51 JHC V, p.646.

which the Commander in Chief gave way to the politicians or vice versa, though in the examples given below it was often a change in military situation which averted a serious clash. In early May Fairfax had been instructed to assemble a force to counter a Royalist uprising on the Scottish border which he was to command.[52] By the middle of the month he was voicing his concern about draining the south of England of troops, but a confrontation was avoided by the uprising in Kent and the decision was not implemented. After the battle of Maidstone the proposal briefly took on new life, but Fairfax's supervision of the siege of Colchester defended by the Kentish insurgents and their Essex supporters meant that he could not be spared, and the Derby House committee sent Cromwell north in his stead.[53]

Another part of England where bad feeling and friction between the military and the politicians showed signs of springing into life was the far south-west of England. In March Fairfax had persuaded parliament that there should be a stronger army presence there because of its record in the First Civil War, but when he sent a regiment to garrison Exeter there was such an uproar in the city that parliament ordered it to be quartered in the surrounding countryside to Fairfax's discomfort if not displeasure. A few months later, however, the boot was on the other foot. In the second week of August when the Scottish army showed signs that it was about to move forward from Cumbria with the Royalist insurgents guarding its left flank against an attack from across the Pennines, Fairfax instructed the New Model Army regiments stationed in the south-west to join the reserve army he was planning to assemble to the north of London. Parliament responded on 8 August by desiring him to rescind the order on the grounds that the King's supporters in Ireland would be encouraged to land troops in Cornwall and incite an uprising there if the regular troops were withdrawn. The Commander in Chief seems to have obeyed but whether he did or not his decision was overtaken by events. The reserve army was no longer needed. Within a fortnight, Cromwell commanding a new force made up of New Model and local regiments, destroyed the Scottish threat for good and for all with his victories at Preston and Winwick.[54]

The interplay between the politicians and the senior commanders juggling with military resources in order to give due weighting to military considerations and the exercise of control by both is perhaps best illustrated by Oliver Cromwell's experience as Fairfax's deputy between April and November 1648. The order for him to assist in putting down the uprising in south Wales had been Fairfax's, which was appropriate as the operation against the insurgents was already under way, but well before he had captured Pembroke Castle, their principal stronghold, the Committee at Derby House on parliament's orders had sent him his new instructions to march north and once there to join Major General John Lambert commanding a mixed bag of provincial and New Model army units. Lambert on his own had been well able to contain local Royalists who had taken over parts of Northumberland and Durham, but before long he could well be facing both a Scottish army and its Royalist allies. Lambert was therefore ordered by the Committee at Derby House after seemingly receiving a paper from Fairfax to avoid a confrontation with the enemy until the reinforcements arrived, but it desired Cromwell to write to him to the same effect in order to drive the point home. After the surrender of Pembroke Castle on 11 July he duly moved quickly north following a demand from the Committee that he should make all possible speed but where the rendezvous was to take place and the direction his brigade was to take to get there was left to him.[55]

52 JHC V, p.555; CSPD 1648–49, p.61.
53 JHL X, pp.266–67 (Fairfax to the House of Lords 19 May 1648); JHC V, p.587; CSPD 1648–49, p.140.
54 CSPD 1648–9, p.208; JHC V, p.663. See also C.H. Firth and G. Davies, *The Regimental History of Cromwell's Army,* 2 vols. (Oxford: the University Press, 1940) II, p.442.
55 CSPD 1648–49, pp.140, 199, 203–04, 208; JHC V, p.650.

After annihilating the Scottish army in mid-August, Cromwell was given the authority to conduct negotiations with the faction of the Scottish nobility which had opposed the invasion of England so as to ensure that there was no further threat from across the border, but once this had been accomplished he remained in the north supervising operations against the English Royalists holed up in Pontefract and Scarborough Castles.[56] Whether this was of his own volition or in response to instructions from Fairfax is uncertain, but the fact that there is no mention of it in the minute book of the Derby House Committee suggests strongly that it was not involved. In November, however, it was on Fairfax's command not that of parliament or its executive committee that Cromwell and most of the New Model regiments under his command joined other detachments in Hertfordshire leaving Lambert in charge of the two sieges.[57]

Actual friction therefore seems to have been minimal during the Second Civil War with the closest parliament and its commander-in-chief came to experiencing an impasse being a spat over the deployment of military resources in the London area. A mob having forced its way into the parliament building the previous August two New Model Army regiments were quartered in Whitehall and its environs at the Two Houses' request to protect them against another such attack, which seemed to be more than a possibility after the serious rioting in the city against New Model Army troops that had taken place in March. In late April, however, Fairfax, having sent Cromwell with several regiments to put down trouble in south Wales, was keen to assemble as large a number of regiments as he could so as to be able to carry out parliament's order to put down the revolt in the north and hopefully discourage a Scottish invasion. He therefore issued orders for the troops guarding parliament to join him whilst fully acknowledging that this was something that required parliament's approval.

On 1 May the House of Commons desired him to rescind the order until such time as it had a replacement in place. This he did but a week later he reminded the members that he needed a quick decision, and that the regiments would be more serviceable for the war effort if he could use them elsewhere. The House began negotiations with the London militia committee for replacements, but there was no sense of urgency. Discussions dragged on for days presumably because on past experience it had concerns about the commitment of any force provided by the city. Fairfax then lost patience and ordered the two regiments to re-join the army, which Colonel Rich's regiment of horse promptly obeyed. The Commons immediately issued a counter-order and Rich may well have returned to Westminster, but within days the worsening security situation in Kent made it abundantly clear that Fairfax would need as large a force of experienced military units as possible to counter it before the insurgents marched on London. But it was not until the very last moment that the House ordered its New Model security force to leave for the army assembly point on Hounslow Heath, though with the added bonus of the New Model regiment garrisoning the Tower of London.[58]

The contrast between the relations between the politicians and the army during the war and those before and immediately afterwards seems remarkable, but it is not difficult to understand. Hindsight makes the campaigns of 1648 look as if parliament's success was a foregone conclusion, but it ignores the perilous situation that informs much of the correspondence between the army 'grandees' and

---

56 JHL X, pp.517–20; C.H. Firth, 'The Clarke Papers' 4 vols., *Camden Society* new series (1891–1901) II, pp.62–63.
57 Wanklyn, *Parliament's Generals*, p.127.
58 H. Cary, *Memorials of the Great Civil War in England* 2 vols. (London: Henry Colburn, 1842) I, pp.393, 413; JHC V, pp. 549–50, 567, 570–71, 573. As late as 26 May the Commons left it to the committee at Derby House to place the regiments wherever it felt fit forcing Fairfax to write the House asking for it to issue an order that they should come to the rendezvous; Cary, *Memorials* I, pp.435–36.

the politicians prior to Cromwell's victories in Lancashire. Uprisings had occurred and were being repressed in more than 10 parts of England and Wales and could be expected elsewhere. Fortunately they were mostly sequential rather than simultaneous, but if they escalated they would force the New Model and the remaining provincial forces at parliament's command to spread themselves too widely, which raised the possibility that they would not be able to come together quickly enough or in sufficient numbers to fight off a Scottish invasion, and this would clearly be so if there was the risk of troops from Ireland and possibly France landing in southern England which would make it necessary for some regiments to remain where they were.

It was therefore a common interest in preserving the constitutional and religious defences against absolutism in church and state, which the revolution of the 1640s had put in place, that caused the coalition in England which had won the first civil war to come together to fight the second. There were spats between what is increasingly irrelevant to describe as Peace and War parties, but they took place largely within the walls of the parliament building and did not impinge on the conduct of the war, though it was probably fortunate that open warfare was done and dusted in the six months between March and August. Once the Scots had been defeated fundamental problems re-emerged namely what to do about the King and what strategy to use for the reconquest of Ireland. The first was progressed if not settled for all time by the second army coup of 6 December 1648 in which the New Model, exasperated by the revival of negotiations with Charles I whom it held responsible for England's woes, created a parliament closer to its concept of a godly legislature by imprisoning over 40 members of the Commons and excluding many more. This was swiftly followed by the trial and execution of the King and the abolition of the monarchy and the House of Lords, but the second problem though it had a hopeful beginning in late 1649 and the first half of 1650 slowed down until the autumn of the following year because of another call on England's military resources, namely the invasion of Scotland.[59]

Safeguarding the Commonwealth 1649-51

With the proclamation of the republic the House of Commons became sovereign in theory as the elected representative of the people of England, or so it claimed in the interests of dignity and decorum though recent events had shown more clearly than ever that this was dependent on the consent of the army.[60] At the same time the Derby House Committee was replaced by the much larger Council of State, which is not surprising as it was to function as the nation's executive with a brief that covered almost every sphere of government. Its members, chosen by the Commons on a yearly basis, were very largely civilians. Only four of the 40 were in the New Model Army – Fairfax, Cromwell, Sir William Constable and Sir Arthur Haselrig – of whom the third and fourth as governors of Gloucester and Newcastle respectively were likely to spend much of their time away from Westminster. Of the generals Fairfax was an intermittent attender even before being deselected in 1650 following his resignation as Commander in Chief, whilst Cromwell was absent on army business for nearly the whole of the time between July 1649 and September 1651.[61] The working members of the council can therefore be comfortably regarded as politicians with the sole restraint on their actions being strict obedience to the House of Commons' instructions past, present and future. The Commons' Journal, however, indicates that parliament had decided to distance itself from matters concerning the defence of the realm unless

---

59   JHC VI, pp.113, 121–27, 166, 168.
60   JHC VI, pp.109–10.
61   JHC VI, p.141. Of the remaining 36 only Phillip Skippon had served in a senior rank in the New Model.

they were of the greatest significance. In other circumstances decisions were delegated to the Council of State.

At its birth the Commonwealth faced many enemies, and it took the New Model three years to rid the British Isles of organised bodies of Stuart loyalists of various hues, but first the Commons and the army had to undergo a similar struggle over strategy and the resources to make it effective that had only been resolved by the First Army Coup of August 1647, and as then Ireland was the focus. In February1649 a coalition of Irish, Ulster Scots and Old and New English pledged to restore the Stuart monarchy had come into being through the efforts of the Marquis of Ormond. This effectively reduced the area under Commonwealth control to a string of ports along the northeast coast and their immediate hinterland. Without substantial military support this was bound to shrink month on month given the number of troops thought to be at the rainbow coalition's disposal, and if assistance did not soon arrive the invasion of England by a predominantly Catholic army intent on overthrowing the republic and extirpating Protestantism would certainly follow.

This was the gist of letters from the commanders at Londonderry, Belfast and Dublin received by parliament on 27 February, and of Cromwell's speech to the Army Council on 23 March described in detail below.[62] The strategy the politicians approved was simple, namely to use brute force to re-establish English hegemony in every corner of the land thus eradicating the threat to the Commonwealth coming from the west, but it was also ambitious and would be costly as it would require a large army to bring it to fruition.[63] However, it was the officers and soldiers of the New Model Army who took the first step in a petition they presented to parliament on 2 March. This as in 1647 listed their gripes about the Commons' failure to respond to their needs and anxieties, but it also demanded that serious, effectual and speedy consideration should be given to the business of Ireland.

The Commons' response to the petition's demand for a strategy to save protestant Ireland was to require the Council of State to hold discussion with the New Model Army commander and his officers and to report back in a week with a firm estimate of the size and cost of the armed forces needed, not only for the conquest of Ireland but also for protecting the republic against its internal foes; four days later the Council reported that it had discussed the forces that were required with General Fairfax and the Army Council. Almost 45,000 troops would be needed to perform both tasks of which 12,000 cavalry, foot and dragoons must be sent to support the units already in Ireland. There was also a clear message that all the regiments for the expeditionary force should come from forces 'now in being'. None should be new ones raised for that purpose.[64]

Parliament and Fairfax and his military advisers were clearly returning to the Peace Party strategy of 1647, but it was as contentious an issue for some officers and many of the rank-and-file as it had been two years before with the additional factor being the conviction of a small but vocal minority that the inhabitants should be left to their own devices. In the words of one officer there were many ways in which an individual might gain salvation and in Ireland too much blood had already been shed in God's name.[65] However, on this occasion time parliament started off on the right foot. It gave an enthusiastic welcome to the petition, described its contents as a moderate set of desires, and undertook to get on with the business of satisfying them immediately so as to allay the petitioners' concerns. It would also

---

62 JHC VI, p.151; Firth ed., 'Clarke Papers' II, p.204.
63 See, for example, Calendar of State Papers Ireland 1647–1660, p.758.
64 JHC VI, pp.153–54, 157. The grievances are not given in full in the Journal, but the headings are to be found in Bulstrode Whitelock, *Memorials of the English Affairs* (London: 1732 ed.), p.385.
65 I. Gentles, *The English Revolution and the Wars in the Three Kingdoms 1638–1652* (Harlow: Pearson, Longman, 2007), pp.385–86; A. Woolrych, *Britain in Revolution* (Oxford: the University Press, 2002), pp.462–63.

enhance the republic's security by discouraging its enemies as they would clearly see that parliament and the army were capable of working happily together for what they saw as the public good.[66]

Whilst parliament began the process of framing legislation to put its promises into effect, the Council of State set up a sub-committee to negotiate with the army over the composition of the force to be sent to Ireland. Cromwell was the member who took on the task of explaining why the New Model should be enthusiastic about taking part in the reconquest of Ireland, but over the next three months it took all his presentational skills followed by some hard bargaining and the suppression of a dangerous revolt before the army was thoroughly committed.

Although informal discussions in the New Model Army as to its contribution towards the expedition to Ireland would have taken place before the presentation of the petition and in the days that followed, the official starting point was Cromwell's address to the Army Council on 23 March. He was extremely cautious and did not dismiss out of hand the possibility of it deciding to play no part at all. However, he stressed at considerable length that the principal danger facing the young republic was Royalist coalition overrunning the whole of Ireland with Scotland and a Royalist uprising in England coming some way behind. At the same time he was in full support of the petition's desires and also of the petitioners' request for guarantees that parliament could raise sufficient money both to satisfy the army's arrears and to cover the expeditionary force's pay whilst it was in Ireland. He also informed the meeting that the Council of State would allow the army to choose which regiments were to go to Ireland, and that he had been offered the post of commander-in-chief but would not formally accept it until he felt the time was right, which he implied would be when their desires had been fully satisfied. Finally he assured his audience that he would obtain a guarantee from parliament that the regiments involved in operations in Ireland would be kept up to strength by recruits from England as their complement shrunk under the pressure of campaigning.[67]

There was, however, one concession to the army which was probably a response to the lack of enthusiasm for fighting overseas. It was not referred to on 23 March, but probably crept in over time or was agreed thereabouts but with an undertaking that to make it public would be a reflection on the army's honour. The Army Council informed the Council of State after the meeting that the expeditionary force should be made up of eight regiments of foot each 1,000 strong, five of cavalry each 600 strong, and 12 troops of dragoons but with the New Model's contribution unspecified. When on 20 April the names of all the New Model regiments went into a hat with a little child charged with dipping in his hand and drawing out those to serve overseas in what the Army Council saw as the fairest method possible, he only drew out nine tickets four for infantry and five for the horse, a total on paper of 7,400 officers and men. By the time the expedition left for Ireland, however, the New Model Army contribution had fallen. The four regiments of foot remained, but there were only two regiments of cavalry and three troops of dragoons commanded by a major rather than four of cavalry and one of dragoons. Between April and August Lambert's regiment had made the case that it should remain in England for security reasons but with 20 men from each troop being used as a recruit for the other cavalry regiments going to Ireland, whilst Scroope's had been disbanded because of its involvement in the mutiny. The reasons for reducing the number of dragoons from six to three has yet to be resolved.[68] Thus, on paper the New Model Army's contribution to the expedition was less than half with the rest of the 12,000

---

66   JHC VI, pp.153–54.
67   Firth ed., 'Clarke Papers', II, pp.200–07.
68   It was probably because of special pleading on Colonel Okey's part. It had nothing to do with the fact that the three troops remaining in England were to be converted into cavalry as this did not happen until a year later: Wanklyn, *Reconstructing the New Model Army* II, p.49.

being either taken from provincial forces like Colonel Phayre's Kentish regiment or raised from scratch in flat contradiction of parliament's resolution in March that all the regiments going to Ireland must be on the army's payroll at that time.[69]

A comment made to the meeting after Cromwell had delivered his speech on 23 March was that the army would be more enthusiastic about contributing regiments for the expedition if he accepted the position of commander in chief. Again he refused to commit himself, and the Army Council did not press him to do so. When the Council of State reported the army's amended list of desires to parliament on 11 April, the document merely requested that all the troops in Ireland should be under the command of a single person. Cromwell probably hoped that his refusing to take the plunge would be interpreted in the army as an honourable act for the reason stated above, and when he did accept his commission in late June it came at a time when almost everything the petitioners wanted was in place apart from ready money.[70] Cromwell, however, had used the long lead-in to increase the powers he could exert in Ireland and to reduce the politicians' capacity to intervene in military operations. Just before agreeing to accept supreme military command there his endeavours were crowned by his appointment as governor general with quasi-viceregal authority in civil government and the right to negotiate with potential defectors and with emissaries sent by the enemy. He then assumed the title Lord Lieutenant in the same way as he assumed that of Lord General of the armies in England on Fairfax's resignation though the previous holders of the office, Fairfax and the Earl of Essex had only been described as such because they already were already holders of peerages. Parliament reacted by saying that he could call himself what he liked. Like the Earl of Strafford in 1640 he also had the right to appoint his deputy, but he did not do so thus avoiding accusations of nepotism. This he intended to be Henry Ireton, his son-in-law, but it was Parliament which made the appointment some days before he accepted his commission as Commander in Chief.[71]

The most likely occasion for a confrontation having passed, it is unsurprising that there was very rarely any friction between parliament and the Council of State on the one hand and the army commanders on the other during the wars in Ireland (1649–52) and in Scotland (1650–51), but this was not entirely a consequence of the shift in the balance of power between the politicians and the generals following the Second Army Coup such that the former were dancing to the latter's tune. Almost all the fighting took place at a distance from Westminster making it unfeasible for the Council of State to intervene directly in operations, and the instruction that pass for strategy as defined above were simply to reconquer the country in the first case and to ensure that the country was not governed by the enemies of the English republic in the second. How this was to be achieved on the ground was left to the General.

Beyond these generalisations there is very little indication of parliament or the Council of State trying to define strategy more closely or to show an inclination to modify it. Their involvement in the plan to create a front in Munster by landing more regiments there than in Dublin in August 1649 may just have come to the fore following news of the major defeat inflicted on the Marquis of Ormond by the Dublin garrison at Rathmines on 2 August, but the fact that the expeditionary force left from Milford Haven rather than Chester is a telling point that it had been some time in the planning. Whether the Council of State knew about it is unclear, but there is no reason why it should have been recorded in the minutes. Secrecy would have been essential as it involved the governor of one of the

---

69 Firth, 'Clarke Papers' II, pp.208–09; Firth and Davies, *Regimental History of the New Model Army* I, pp. 255, 296; Firth and Davies, *Regimental History*, II, p. 655; Wanklyn, *Reconstructing the New Model Army*, I, pp.104, 108, 255; Wanklyn, *Reconstructing the New Model Army*, II, pp.179–82, 190–99.
70 JHC VI, pp.176, 239.
71 CSPD 1649-50, p.198; JHC VI, pp.234, 239, 242, 247.

ports on the southern coast of Ireland declaring allegiance to the Commonwealth for it to have been feasible.[72] However, surely members of the council would have asked questions had the soldiers tried to keep them in the dark as Milford Haven was the wrong place from which to send reinforcements to the garrisons in Leinster and Ulster held by the Commonwealth's friends.[73]

As for the reactive as opposed to pro-active face of strategy parliament and its council had little incentive to try and impose a new plan on their generals as in neither Scotland nor Ireland did English troops suffer a major operational setback or disaster. There is, however, evidence of the Council of State trying to achieve a change of course in Scotland in April 1651 after six months of stalemate since the victory at Dunbar caused by the strength of the Scots' defences at Stirling which made an advance beyond the Firth of Forth impossible, but it was both tentative and tactful. Its letter to Cromwell also carried the clear implication that the army not parliament was by then the final arbiter of strategy. The Council suggested to Ireton, who was commanding the army in Ireland in the Lord General's absence, that he might help end the impasse by landing troops on the west coast of Scotland and thus force the Scottish generals to reduce the strength of their troops defending Stirling and give Cromwell the chance of making a breakthrough. Ireton and Cromwell were to discuss the matter and, being the men on the spot parliament would respect their decision. This was a strategy for defeating the Scots which had been suggested several times during the course of the First and Second Bishops' Wars in the late 1630s,[74] but in 1651 it seems not even to have reached the planning stage.

Indirect evidence that the army was the arbiter in strategic matters is seen in the unbelievable patience shown by the Council of State and parliament with the situation at Stirling given the heavy expense of maintaining an army of 16,000 men in Scotland, which on paper rose to well over 20,000 by the summer of 1651, and the slow roll-out of the scheme Cromwell had approved for solving the problem. The strategic plan was to bypass the lines of Stirling by landing troops on the open shore on the far side of the Firth of Forth and after they had captured the port of Burntisland to fill Fife with English troops thus forcing the Scots to come out and fight or else to flee. The difficulty was that the first stage of the required many flat-bottomed boats which had to be specially constructed in England and then sailed to Leith, the principal port on the south side of the Firth. Instead of complaining or dropping hints the council accepted at face value information from the army that the boats equipped with removable keels were not seaworthy enough to sail to Scotland until the late spring, and that as they needed to hug the shore Royalist-held castles along the Scottish east coast must first be captured to prevent their being blown out of the water.[75] Its only action during the eight months' wait was to urge Cromwell to return to England for a spell and appoint a deputy when he fell ill in June – an offer he declined – and when it followed this up by sending doctors to Scotland to treat him it was almost

---

72   For the difficulties of landing an army on an open shore see Wanklyn, 'Oliver Cromwell's generalship and the conquest of Scotland', *Cromwelliana*, series 3 no. 4, pp.37–47.

73   The instigator may have been Lord Lisle, who was a member of the Council of State, and whom Little has shown had been in close contact with Cromwell for several years. He had also commanded an expedition to Munster in 1647, and with his knowledge of his province and the English officers in command there he probably first put the idea into the minds of the soldiers and/ or the politicians that the garrison at Youghal might change sides when the ships carrying the expeditionary force first appeared on the horizon; Little, 'Cromwell and Ireland', pp.124–36; JHC VI, p.141.

74   CSPD 1651, p.163; M. Wanklyn, *The Army of Occupation in Ireland 1603–1642* (Solihull: Helion and co., 2022), pp. 141–44, 152–57 shows that Strafford was less keen on the idea than has previously been claimed.

75   Wanklyn,' Cromwell's Generalship and the Conquest of Scotland' 1650–1651', pp.40–46.

certainly an act of kindness rather than an attempt to find out if he was exaggerating the seriousness of his illness to cover up his lack of operational imagination.[76]

Supplying all their armies with sufficient men and materials to secure parliament's strategic objectives had been a perennial cause of friction between the executive and its generals when the war was being fought on several fronts. There is, however, no sign of this in the war in Scotland as there was only a single front for almost the whole time, and when Lambert in December 1650 and July 1651 and George Monck in August 1651 were briefly in charge of formations operating at a distance from the main army, they were well able to bring their operations to a successful conclusion without calling on the council for additional resources that were earmarked for Cromwell's troops. However, there was an opportunity for a row involving Ireton, Cromwell and the council when Ireton discovered that supplies intended for the army in Ireland had been sent to Scotland, but he had three good reasons for not making a fuss: he had married the new Captain General's daughter; they had been a close political associates since 1644; and as commissary general of horse in the New Model and deputy lieutenant in Ireland he had Cromwell as his superior officer twice over.[77]

When all is said and done in 1649–52 as in 1648 defence of the homeland was an overarching concern which at times caused parliament and its executive committee to assert themselves. The early experience of Colonel Hacker's regiment can serve as an illustration of interference at the regimental level. Cromwell's expedition having left for Ireland in August short of two and a half regiments of horse was allotted it as a replacement but in October the Council of State asked him not to order it to come to Ireland till the spring because of concerns about Royalist unrest in England. When early in the new year intelligence suggested that the unrest would be more widespread than originally thought, the council informed him that it could not let it leave. Cromwell then apparently asked it to require Fairfax to dispatch three New Model Army troops to Ireland instead to enable him to complete his son Henry's newly formed regiment, but the council told Sir Thomas Fairfax that he should send provincial formations. The Lord General compromised. Cromwell duly received New Model Army units but two of them were dragoons whilst the third was the troop that Henry had previously commanded in Colonel Harrison's cavalry regiment.[78]

A year later there were fears about an uprising in Lancashire which would receive aid from Scotland to which the Council of State responded by sending north New Model Army troops stationed in England. Cromwell was not offended by an order that should have come from him, but he recommended that they should be stationed at Carlisle where he could easily reinforce them if necessary.[79] Nothing came of the rumour, but a strategically and operationally significant example of the Council of State coming to life in defence of the homeland occurred in August 1651 when serious fighting in England became a reality. In the previous month sufficient landing craft having at last arrived at Leith Cromwell launched a highly successful assault on the south shore of the Firth of Forth which General Lambert followed up with a decisive victory at Inverkeithing over a division of the Scottish army intent on driving the English into the sea. Immediately afterwards General Monck captured the deepwater port of Burntisland and Cromwell crossed the Firth of Forth into Fife with most of his army intent

---

76 CSPD 1651, pp.218, 236.
77 *Oxford Dictionary of National Biography*, vol. 29.
78 Firth and Davies, *Regimental History* I, pp. 110–14, 231; CSPD 1649–50, pp.329, 391; CSPD 1650, p.51; Wanklyn, *Reconstructing the New Model Army* II, pp.50–51, 190–97.
79 CSPD 1651, pp.34–35, 102–03, 136; Abbott, *Cromwell's Letters and Speeches* II, pp.411–12.

on capturing Perth, which would cut the army at Stirling off from the rest of the country that was still under Royalist control. The operation in Fife, however, left the door to England wide open.[80]

When the Commander in Chief and his correspondents at Westminster were discussing the possibility of an invasion of England earlier in the year they were thinking of a 'flying' brigade of cavalry and mounted infantry like that expected to go to the assistance of the Lancashire insurgents not the entire Scottish army, but this is what happened, and he had some explaining to do. In a letter written to the council at Leith on 4 August he claimed that he had not been taken by surprise, but that there was no alternative to crossing the Firth of Forth and invading Fife in force. If he had continued to play the Scots at their own game hoping that their guard would eventually slip, he might wait forever whilst his army mouldered away around him. In his opinion it would no longer be in a fit state to defend of the Commonwealth if it spent another winter in Scotland.[81]

Unfortunately he had not had enough soldiers under his command to both defeat the forces from Stirling in battle if they marched north or to bar their passage if they moved in the opposite direction, but the large body of mounted troops he had left in the Edinburgh area commanded by General Harrison joined in due course by General Lambert's cavalry regiments shipped back to Leith would be sufficiently pro-active to harass and thus slow down their progress, or to stop it altogether at pinch points such as the bridges over the Ribble and the Mersey if they took the west coast route or the Tyne and the Tees should they march parallel to the North Sea coast and then into Yorkshire. Delaying tactics would thus give him time to catch the enemy up with the rest of his army whereupon he would take his revenge. In the meantime parliament should organise the county militias of the north to assist the mounted troops in their task of delaying the Scottish advance.

The advice showed Cromwell's concern as commander in chief for the defence of the homeland, but the Council of State had heard of the Scottish march south almost before Cromwell had, and preparations to resist the enemy were well under way before the letter reached London.[82] Nevertheless it injected an element of urgency into the activities of the Council of State and the House of Commons. With the Scottish army now located between the capital and Cromwell's infantry and possibly his cavalry they would be foolhardy to place their whole trust in his optimistic analysis, and the council therefore set about assembling its own army commanded by Lieutenant General Fleetwood beginning with the few New Model units stationed in southern and central England. They were to rendezvous first at Barnet and then at Northampton where they would be joined by the militias of counties from Cheshire southwards. However, the situation became much more serious when Cromwell's operational plan for the defence of England began to unravel.[83]

On 19 August the forces the Commander in Chief had sent ahead in conjunction with the Cheshire militia regiments tried but failed to stop the Scots crossing the Mersey, whereupon the enemy's speed of march accelerated. By the following day they were at Stone eight miles to the north of Stafford and believed to be heading for Lichfield which was uncomfortably close to the high road to London. Moreover, Cromwell and his infantry were making slower progress than had been anticipated. The Council of State therefore ordered its forces to assemble at Coventry, which would give them the chance of attacking the flank of the Scottish army or blocking its path anywhere along the 25 mile stretch of

---

80   CSPD 1651, pp.102–03.
81   Cary, *Memorials of the Civil Wars* II, pp. 288–90, 291–93.
82   JHC VI, pp. 614–15, 616–17; Whitelock, *Memorials*, pp.500–02.
83   CSPD 1651, pp 328, 344.

Watling Street as it swung in an arc from east to south-east on the Warwickshire/ Northamptonshire border.

The Council of State also overruled the commanders of Cromwell's advance guard. Lambert and Harrison had headed east from the Mersey crossing to Congleton with the aim of joining the Lord General at Sheffield, a classical tactic of falling back on a larger friendly force after suffering a setback, but it is not clear whether this was on their own initiative or in obedience to instructions from Cromwell. Instead they were ordered to move to Coventry, but even after the addition of experienced cavalry regiments to a force consisting primarily of infantry, the council was worried. It had little information about Cromwell's movements and feared that the farther south the Scots marched the more likely would it be for them to ignite insurrections in the support of the Stuart monarchy. The command structure also must have caused concern given Fleetwood's lack of experience in commanding anything larger than a regiment. To ensure that there were no misunderstandings or mistakes on the part of the senior officers the council therefore decided to send a subcommittee to Coventry. It was also charged with gathering intelligence, encouraging the troops and facilitating communications between the capital and the army. All in all it looks like a reversion to the experiment for civilian control tried in the autumn of 1644.[84]

Within few hours, however, the clouds began to clear. The Scottish army had changed the direction of its march from south-east to due south. The danger to London thus receded but not that of a major uprising in Worcestershire, Herefordshire and south-east Wales, which had been predominately Royalist in sympathy in the First Civil War. However, it became clear a few days later not only that the Scottish army was too exhausted to continue its march beyond Worcester but also that Cromwell and his infantry would shortly join Lambert, Harrison and Fleetwood in central Warwickshire where they would be well-placed to block the road from Worcester to London. At that point the Council of State took a back seat allowing the lord general to plan and execute the complex operation that would culminate in the total destruction of the Scottish army at Worcester on 3 September.

A Narrative of the Control of Command 1642-51

There is no doubt from the wording of the Earl of Essex's commission as Commander in Chief that he was ultimately under the control of his political masters, but whether this control was to be exercised only as a last resort or to be a matter of routine was not spelled out. They certainly kept strategy for themselves as shown by their attempt first to end the war before it began and then to talk to the queen about a negotiated peace both of which impeded hopeful military operations, but the extent to which they interfered with operations that were under way either by direct commands or through MPs and peers holding commissions in Essex's army cannot be determined with any degree of certainty because the minutes and correspondence of the Committee of Safety, which acted as parliament's war cabinet between August 1642 and February 1644, no longer exist.

The temptation to intervene in operational matters must, however, have been intense when the Commander in Chief did not win the war quickly, but in the summer of 1643 he blamed this on the failure to provide him with sufficient resources to carry out their strategic plan to chase the King's army from Oxford whilst not disciplining Sir William Waller, regarded widely as a more enterprising

---

84 CSPD 1651, pp.344–45, 347, 348–55; Whitelock, *Memorials*, p.503. During the days of crisis parliament did nothing of a military nature other than listen to the various letters the Council of State had received from the army commanders and return them to the council without comment: JHC VII, pp.1–7.

general, for disobeying his orders. Nevertheless Essex's reputation revived after a successful campaign to relieve Gloucester in September 1643, which he had recommended as the best possible option for regaining the strategic initiative, followed by a defensive victory at Newbury in September where he fought the King's army to a standstill. He gained his reward in the guise of operational control over Waller's army, but squandered the opportunity for consolidating his control over provincial armies by doing nothing during the winter months whilst his rivals Waller and also the earl of Manchester commanding the army of the Eastern Association enhanced their respective reputations for boldness and administrative competence.

The appointment of the Committee of Both Kingdoms in February 1644 following the alliance of parliament with the Scots was a clear sign that the politicians, probably following a determined push from its allies, were determined to win the war quickly by formalising and enhancing their control over the operations their generals were to conduct to implement the strategies their new war cabinet devised. Orders and counter-orders issued by the Committee followed one another in quick succession and friction quickly ensued. By later summer all three generals had lost patience with commands which they saw as misconceived, impractical or even positively dangerous intervention in the running of the war and began to go their own way. When Essex and Manchester's conduct of operations in contravention of the committee's orders caused concern at Westminster about parliament's ability to defend itself against Royalist resurgence in the south of England it devised a scheme for micromanagement of operations and even tactics. The three generals, whose armies were now working together to stem the Royalist tide only 30 miles from London in what would be the last campaign of the year, were ordered to accept two of the Committee as members of an eight-member council of war with authority to overrule the military men's recommendations through their daily correspondence with their fellows at Westminster. However, the experiment was not repeated as it did not prevent the campaign ending in stalemate with the King's forces still in control of most of England south of the Thames.

The reforms of the winter of 1644–45, which saw the three generals replaced by Sir Thomas Fairfax and the New Model created out of the best elements in their armies, did nothing to change the way in which the Committee of Both Kingdoms interfered with operations during the new campaigning season, but the confusion that resulted by early June from its orders ended in its giving up any attempt to control operations, which became the responsibility of the Commander in Chief advised by his council of war but with parliament still having a handle on strategy and troop movements. This change removed much of the friction that had characterised relations between the generals and their political masters since 1642. It also made a contribution towards final victory over the King in April 1646, but some of the causes of friction had been repressed rather than eliminated and could easily re-emerge when circumstances changed – were the generals competent or loyal enough to deliver on the strategies determined by politicians, and if not how were they to be brought into line or disciplined? However, the next confrontation between the generals and the politicians came about over strategy and how it was to be carried out not while it was in the process of being implemented via operations.

The first serious attempt by the army to deprive parliament of control over strategy followed the announcement in March 1647 of the Peace Party's plans for reconquering Ireland the effect of which would be to cheat and humiliate the army at a time when it expected its grievances concerning back pay in particular were to be addressed. After three months of growing friction the attempt by the politicians to impose their will on the army's without having the means to resist if the army fought back resulted in widespread mutinies which it had no physical means of suppressing. Order was restored in August by the army in a coup, and it quickly replaced parliament's plans for reconquering Ireland with its own thus creating a precedent for future claims that it had a veto over any strategies devised by the politicians.

When civil war broke out in England again in 1648 army and parliament worked together using very similar conventions to those put in place in 1645, but the second army coup of December 1648, which created a parliament dominated by the army's supporters, and the subsequent negotiations between army and parliament about the resources that were required for the reconquest of Ireland made it very clear that the former had ultimate control over both strategy and operations in normal conditions. Neither parliament nor its executive committee the Council of State therefore played much part in the conduct of the wars in Ireland and Scotland that followed, though there were other factors at work such as distance and the good relationships of the generals in charge with one another, but on occasions when it considered that the homeland was threatened the Council had recourse to its reversionary powers and exerted itself.

But that was not quite the end of the story of parliament's loss of control over the conduct of war. Less than two years later Cromwell accompanied by several files of musketeers sent it packing and he and his senior officers assumed full sovereign powers which had been theirs in embryo since 1647. The reasons for his actions were complex, and they have caused endless debates at the time and since, but one factor was the army's dissatisfaction with the progress of the war parliament had declared on the Netherlands in 1651 as this swallowed up money which should have been used for paying its wages, now heavily in arrears as in 1647.[85] However, modern scholarship downplays Royalist claims that one of parliament's reasons for seeking a confrontation with the Dutch was to distract the army from making another foray into the field of politics. Nevertheless, Cromwell's action had removed 'the one shred of legality with which it had hitherto covered its actions. Henceforth military force must appear in its proper shape'.[86]

Malcolm Wanklyn
February 2023

---

85 Woolrych, *Britain in Revolution*, pp 526–27.
86 C. H. Firth, *Cromwell* (London: Putnam and co., 1904 ed.), p.324.

"For Suppressing Any Forraigne Invasion, Intestine Trouble or Insurrection"[1]
Fortress Scotland – 1650–1707 from the 2019 National Army Museum conference

David Flintham

Introduction

The Civil Wars in Scotland ended, as they did elsewhere across the British Isles, with the reduction of the remaining Royalist strongholds. Although Edinburgh itself fell soon after the disaster at Dunbar on 3 September 1650, Edinburgh Castle, so long the symbol of Royal authority in Scotland, held out until December when it was betrayed to the English.[2] Tantallon Castle, 30 miles east of Edinburgh, threatened Oliver Cromwell's lines of communication and so was besieged and taken by General George Monck, supported by the Navy, in February 1651. Monck was then given the responsibility of subduing the rest of Scotland, taking Stirling on 14 August 1651 and Dundee less than three weeks later, although Dunnottar Castle held out until May 1652. But the reduction of these strongholds did not bring peace to Scotland, and as a result, the Protectorate Government[3] turned its attention to how to control Scotland and thus heralded a century of military 'policing'.

Whilst the principle concern was the Highlands, the Lowlands also experienced periods of disturbance (the Covenanter rebellions of 1666 and 1679, the so called 'Killing Time', between 1680 and 1688, and the failed rising in 1685 by Archibald Campbell, 9th Earl of Argyll). Though this did not result in the construction of new fortresses, it meant that Dumbarton, Edinburgh, and Stirling Castles (the latter two sitting high on their volcanic outcrops) retained larger garrisons than they might, had areas of potential unrest been restricted purely to the Highlands.

Thus, Scotland needed to look at its internal defences to a far great extent than that needed in England. The existing castles were vulnerable to artillery, with the result that they were improved with the addition of 'state-of-the-art' defences (a challenge to the military engineers of the time), whilst internally, the accommodation would have to be remodelled into barracks. In addition, to counter the new danger, barracks were constructed and garrisons were established at strategic locations.

---

1   1663 Militia Act of the Scottish Parliament in T. Thomson and C. Innes (eds.), *Acts of the Parliaments of Scotland*, (Edinburgh, 1820), volume 7, p.481.
2   K. Corsar, 'The Surrender of Edinburgh Castle, December 1650', *The Scottish Historical Review*, (1949), n. 28, pp.43–54.
3   Whilst the Protectorate didn't actually come into being into December 1653, the term is used here to describe English rule in Scotland for the entire period of English occupation during the 1650s.

At the Restoration, the military landscape of Scotland was dominated by the vestiges of the English occupation of the previous decade, namely the great Protectorate citadels. And it was from the citadel at Leith that Monck would commence the journey that would lead ultimately to the Restoration of Charles II. Thus, the story of how Scotland was fortified during the second half of the seventeenth century starts with these great citadels.

The Protectorate Citadels

Whilst not many Scots had welcomed Cromwell's invasion and subsequent occupation, few could have argued that the peace it brought with it was such that 'a man may ride all Scotland over with a switch in his hand and £100 in his pocket, which he could not have done these 500 years'.[4] But this peace came at a price, and it took an army of some 36,000 men to achieve. The cost of maintaining this level of military presence was untenable, but the solution was a stroke of military genius, and one which was to dominate Scottish military thinking for the next 100 years. Five citadels were built at key strategic locations enabling a reduction in military numbers, and requiring a policing force of just 10,000 to maintain, but sufficient to maintain a firm grip on a still unhappy, and potentially rebellious country. One citadel was built at Ayr on the south-west Scottish coast, two more (Inverness and a smaller fort at Inverlochy, now Fort William) at either end of the Great Glen, one at St. Johnstone (Perth), and the final one at Leith, on the Firth of Forth close to Edinburgh.

Construction of the citadels at Ayr, Inverness and St. Johnstone were all started in the spring of 1652, but those at Inverlochy and Leith were not started until the middle of the decade (the latter replacing a more temporary fort which was constructed in the first few months of the English occupation). These defensive structures also served as barracks[5] for garrisons who would police the local districts. The English could not afford to underestimate the Scots and their experience of fortifications – during 1644–46, the Scottish Army of the Solemn League and Covenant had amassed a great deal of experience at siege warfare during their campaigns in England, whilst during the Third Civil War, the Scottish Royalist forces had employed field fortifications.[6] The English Commonwealth, therefore, resolved to build these Citadels in the latest formidable style and their size alone, containing barracks and administrative buildings, had not been seen in Scotland since the largest French forts of the previous century. Each citadel was different in size, shape and layout. The citadels were well placed, according to Monck, 'to suppress disorders and obviate dangers',[7] and controlled the Highlands better than the Scots or English had done before.

In addition to these major fortresses, 20 other smaller garrisons were established across the country, which, by 1653, included: Dundee, Aberdeen, Inchgarvie, Linlithgow, Dumbarton, Stirling, Burntisland, Tantallon Castle, Bass ('Rock') Island, Inchkeith, Ruthven Castle, Braemar, Blair Atholl, Dunkeld, Brodick and Dunnottar Castles, Dunstaffnage, Dunnolly, and Orkney. In addition, were also

---

4 A. A. Tait, 'The Protectorate Citadels of Scotland', *Architectural History: Journal of the Society of Architectural Historians of Great Britain*, (1965), Vol. 8, p.9 (https://www.jstor.org/stable/1568268?seq=1/subjects, accessed 16/02/2019).
5 C. H. Firth, *Scotland and the Protectorate. Letters and Papers relating to the military government from January 1654 to June 1659*, (Edinburgh: Scottish History Society, 1899), pp.xxxix-li, and C. H. Firth, *Cromwell's Army*, (London: 1962), p.294n.
6 http://www.fortified-places.com/worcester.html (accessed 16/02/2019).
7 Firth, *Scotland and the Protectorate*, p.304.

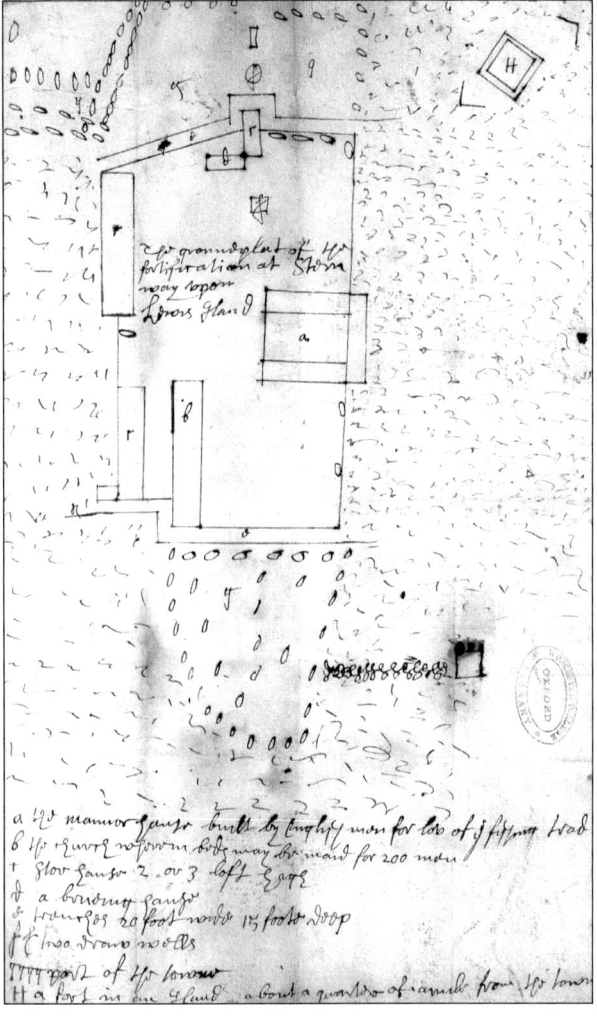

drawn up for a fort on Shetland, although this wasn't constructed.[8]

There was another fort built at Stornoway on the island of Lewis in the Outer Hebrides. Built in 1653 on the orders of Colonel Robert Lilburne, Monck's successor, its purpose was not only controlling the local population (especially the local Earl of Seaforth, known for his Royalist sympathies), but also to prevent Stornoway becoming a Dutch base.[9] According to a plan held in the Clarke papers,[10] the fort enclosed an existing manor house. The exact location and layout of the fort is a matter of conjecture.[11]

Following its capture by the English on Christmas Eve, 1650, Cromwell ordered further strengthening of the defences of Edinburgh Castle, including the construction of a hornwork ahead of the defences surrounding the castle's entrance. This feature, built on the site of an earlier defence known as the 'Spur',[12] comprised of a pair of demi-bastions, positioned either side of a length of curtain wall, and fronted by a ditch and counterscarp. In 1679, it was

A plan (c.1653) of the fort constructed in Stornoway on the Island of Lewis in the Outer Hebrides. (The Provost and Fellows of Worcester College, Oxford)

8 C. H. Firth (ed.), *Scotland and the Commonwealth*, (Edinburgh: Scottish History Society, 1895), pp.116–8, and Stewart Cruden, *The Scottish Castle*, (Edinburgh: Spurbooks, 1981), pp.226–7.
9 E. Patricia Dennison and Russel Coleman, *Historic Stornoway*, The Scottish burgh survey, (Edinburgh: Historic Scotland, 1997), pp.24–5. For a description of the Cromwellian conquest and occupation of Stornoway see Willie Foulger, 'Roundheads in Lewis', *Sy Gone By*, (Stornoway: Stornoway Historical Society, 2019).
10 William Clarke (1623?–66) was Secretary of War to both the Commonwealth and Charles II. His son, George Clarke, donated his father's papers, which included plans of several of the Commonwealth fortresses, to Worcester College in Oxford.
11 In early 2019, a stone wall almost 3m (10ft) thick and 2m (6ft) high was discovered during work to add an extension to a Stornoway Port Authority office. Archaeologists believe it formed part of the Cromwellian defensive rampart. https://www.bbc.co.uk/news/amp/uk-scotland-highlands-islands-48364674 (accessed 22/05/2019).
12 Until 1649, the approach to Edinburgh Castle across what is now the Esplanade was protected by a feature known as the 'Spur', dating from c.1548. This was removed in 1649 to make way for improved artillery defences.

described as 'a dry ditch walled in both sides with a parapet or breastwork within for planting guns and a glassis without'.¹³

St. Johnstone

The citadel at St. Johnstone was planned and begun by Major General Richard Deane in the spring of 1652. Deane wasn't regarded as a military engineer as such (he was an artilleryman, and had commanded the New Model Army's artillery at Naseby), and this might explain why of all the citadels, it is the simplest, taking the form of a square with a bastion at each corner. It was constructed to the south of the town, and following the Restoration: 'Royal Charters: King Charles [II]. Charter by King Charles [II] granting to the magistrates and inhabitants of the burgh of Perth the Citadel built on the south peninsula (Inch) of the said burgh with all the arms etc therein'. [Tag with Great Seal].¹⁴

The 1668 *Compt Book* of Bailie Alexander Jamieson, merchant in Perth and sometime town treasurer, records the disposal of the material of the citadel following its demolition,¹⁵ although enough of it survived for it to be incorporated into the town's defences when the town was fortified by the Jacobites in 1715¹⁶.

Ayr

Ayr Citadel, in south-west Scotland, was also founded by Deane in the spring of 1652, and was designed 'against England's enemies for England's friend, whom ever God protect' by Hans Ewald Tessin, who was of Swedish origin,¹⁷ and

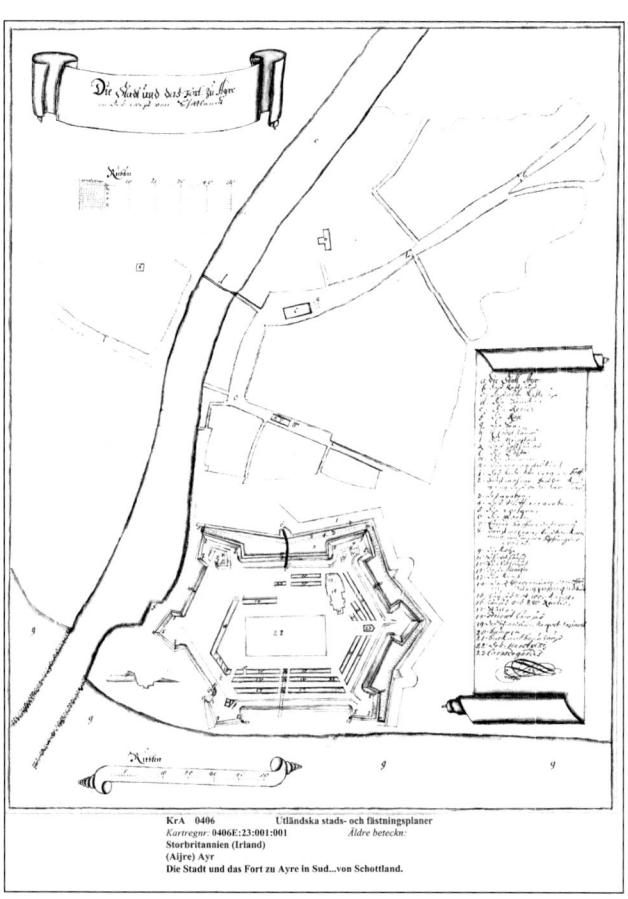

Ewald Tessin's *The City and the Fort in Ayre in Sud ... of Scotland*, c.1652. (Swedish National Archives – Krigsarkivet/Utländska stads- och fästningsplaner)

13 R. S. Mylne, *The Master Masons to the Crown of Scotland and their Works* (Edinburgh: Scott, Ferguson and Burness, 1893), pp.204–5.
14 Perth & Kinross Council Archive, *Perth Burgh Records*, B59/23/35.
15 Perth & Kinross Council Archive, *Burgh finances*, B59/25/1/11.
16 Lewis Petit, *A Plan of Perth with the Retrenchment made about it by the Pretenders Engineers*, (1716).
17 https://www.st-andrews.ac.uk/history/ssne/item.php?id=6600&id2=6600 (accessed 30/12/2019).

was chief engineer of the New Model Army (on his plan of 1654, Tessin signs himself as 'military architect'). Situated where the river Ayr entered the Firth of Clyde, of all the citadels built in Scotland during the 1650s, Ayr Citadel was the most accomplished, although in 1653, Lilburne reported that the plan 'was a most stately things and very strong but a great deal too large and costly to maintain'.[18]

Its main axis ran north to south, and took the form of a symmetrical elongated hexagon, with a bastion at each angle. Protected by rivers on two sides, its remaining two landward fronts were protected by a floodable outer ditch, and additionally protected by a covered way with re-entrant place of arms, and a sloping earthwork glacis. The seaward-side bastions were smaller than the landward ones. Access to the ramparts and its terreplein (fighting platform) was provided by broad ramps, notably to the north, which might have accommodated a mortar battery. The north-east bastion was surmounted by a prominent cavalier (raised gun battery).

Internally, the citadel was equally impressive – its large size permitted a raised centrally planned parade square (this was termed 'market place' in the original drawings). On three sides of this square were a carefully laid out range of buildings, including barracks and also administrative buildings. The fourteenth century St. John's Kirk was incorporated into the citadel at one corner of the parade square.

Ayr Citadel today. (Undiscovered Scotland)

18 Quoted in Cruden, p.231.

It is likely that the citadel was designed to accommodate a garrison of up to 1,000 men, although it is unknown whether this was ever achieved.[19] After the Restoration the citadel was slighted, although approximately half of the perimeter wall survived albeit not to the original height, as have some of the earth ramparts, and thus is the best preserved of the citadels.

Inverness

In 1652, Deane founded a citadel in Inverness at the northern end of the Great Glen. However, little seems to have progressed until the following year, and a request was made for Joachim Hane, a German-born engineer, to supervise the laying of the foundation. Unfortunately, Hane was otherwise engaged in France and England, so it is likely that John Rosworm attended instead (and in 1659, Rosworm was nominated to Parliament as Engineer General of the Army).[20] Whilst local labour was employed to undertake the digging, skilled labour came from England. The fort was finally completed in 1657 at an enormous cost in excess of £500,000.

Known as 'Oliver's Fort', its plan was a large regular pentagon with a bastion at each corner. Located on the east bank of the River Ness, the west side of the citadel was protected by the river, the others by a flooded ditch which was capable of taking boats. Further out, the citadel was protected by existing marshes.

The minister of Kirkhill, whilst admiring Inverness citadel, considered it a 'sacrilegious structure and could not stand' as it was constructed from stones robbed from several near-by ecclesiastical buildings including Kinloss Abbey, Beauly Priory, and St. Mary's Church in Inverness. He described the citadel thus:

> It was five cornered with bastions, with a wide trench that an ordinary barque might sait in a full tide; the breast-work three storeys, built of hewn stone limed within, and a brick wall. Centinel houses of stone at each corner, a sally-port to the south leading to the town, and on the north a great entry or gate called the Port, with a strong drawbridge of oak, called the Blue Bridge … this bridge was drawn evry night, and a strong guard within … In the centre of the citadel stood a great four-square building, all hewn stone, called the magazine and granary. In the third storey was the church, well furnished with a stately pulpit and seats, a wide bartizan at top, and a brave great clock with four large gilded dials and a curious ball … North-west and north-east are lower storeys for ammunition, timber, lodgings for manufactories, stablings, provision and brewing houses, and a great long tavern.[21]

Leith

There were two citadels at Leith.[22] The first was built sometime between 1650 and 1652 and was the work of the mason John Mylne (the younger). It was a square design with a bastion at each corner. It was in use for several years – as late as 1655, Monck as the Commander in Chief in Scotland, was still

---

19   http://old.scotwars.com/Ayr_citadel.htm (accessed 16/02/2019).
20   Letter of General Monck to the Protector, August 1654, quoted in Firth, *Scotland and the Protectorate*, p.163, and Cruden, p.233.
21   The minister of Kirkhill writing in 1655, in in Firth, *Scotland and the Protectorate*, pp.XLIV–XLVI.
22   This was not the first time that Leith had been fortified – in 1560 it was fortified by the French (at the time it was the most modern fortification to be found anywhere in the country) and besieged by the English. See

funding its maintenance.[23] It was not until 26 May 1656 that work began on the new citadel, built on the site of the former fort. According to William Maitland, writing in 1753, it was pentagonal in shape with a bastion at each corner and one gateway, facing east.[24] It cost the local population (who were forced to pay for its construction) an estimated £10,000[25] – not surprisingly, funding was an issue and in 1657–8, a deficit of £1,800 was reported to the House of Commons.[26] It became Monck's headquarters and he considered it to be exceedingly strong and easy to defend and could be relieved by sea if necessary. In a letter to Cromwell dated 11 July 1657 to support a request for funds to assist with the completion of the building, he assures the Lord Protector that there can always be six feet of water in the moat 'so that it cannot be undermined and, if the enemy should make a gallery over it, he may let in the water and destroy it at pleasure'.[27]

The remains of Leith Citadel. (David Flintham)

David Flintham, 'The Fortifications of Leith, 1558–1916', in *Fort*, (Fortress Study Group, 2013), Volume 41, pp.92–99.
23   Frances Dow, *Cromwellian Scotland*, (Edinburgh: John Donald Publishers, 1999), p.142.
24   Royal Commission on the Ancient and Historical Monuments of Scotland, Canmore ID 51917, Site Number NT27NE 10.
25   Michael Fry, *Edinburgh: A History of the City*, (London: Macmillan, 2010), p.170, and Peter Gaunt, *The Cromwellian Gazetteer*, (Gloucester: Alan SuttonPublishing, 1987), p.208.
26   Dow, p.219.
27   Cruden, p.233.

Leith was perhaps the greatest of the five citadels, 'one of best fortifications that ever we beheld, passing fair and sumptuous', according to John Ray who viewed the citadel in 1661.[28] Monck was aware of the long-standing rivalry between Leith and Edinburgh and was anxious to promote Leith's 'trade which, he claimed, was obstructed by the historic privileges of the city of Edinburgh',[29] later adding that Leith Citadel was there to 'keepe in awe the chief citty of this nation'.[30]

On 10 September 1658, a salute was fired from the Citadel to mark the proclamation of Richard Cromwell as Lord Protector,[31] yet less than a year later, Monck was instructing Jeremy Smith to secure Leith Citadel[32] and at the end of 1659, as Monck prepared to march south and secure the Restoration of Charles II, he left Major General Thomas Morgan in command.[33]

At the Restoration in 1660, the garrison was temporarily retained, in case there was a need to suppress any attempt at armed resistance to the return of Charles II.

Inverlochy

The Great Glen's strategic importance had been recognised as early as the thirteenth century, with the result that curtain-walled castles were built at Duart, Dunstaffnage, Inverlochy, Urquhart and Inverness. This fact was not overlooked by Cromwell during the 1650s, and in addition to the citadel built at Inverness, a smaller, more modest earthwork artillery fort was built at Inverlochy, on a promontory at the point where the River Nevis enters Loch Linnhe. According to a plan held in the Clarke Papers[34] examined by Stewart Cruden, the fort was surrounded on all sides by water thanks to a zig-zag trench which cut across the fort's landward side. The fort itself had one full three-pointed bastion at its south-east corner which covered the trench. This irregular enceinte had demi-bastions at its other four angles.[35]

Conditions for the garrison were hard and disagreeable even for professional soldiers accustomed to privation, and service at Inverlochy was regarded as so severe and unpleasant that the garrison was composed of one company drawn by lot from each regiment of foot in Scotland, so that there should be no suspicion of favouritism or prejudice; and these companies were changed annually.[36]

The Return of the King

In the weeks following Monck's departure at the beginning of 1660, the forces in Scotland were centred on Inverness, Perth, Leith, and Stirling, under the command of Morgan (who was later to become Major General Sir Thomas Morgan), who had accompanied Monck as far as York before returning to Scotland.[37]

---

28 Cruden, p.234.
29 Maurice Ashley, *General Monck*, (London: Jonathan Cape Ltd, 1977), p.141.
30 Tait, Vol. 8, p.9.
31 Dow, p.233.
32 Ashley, p.163.
33 John Childs, *The Army of Charles II*, (London: Routledge and Kegan Paul, 1976), p.196.
34 William Clarke (1623?–66) was Secretary of War to both the Commonwealth and Charles II. His son, George Clarke, donated his father's papers, which included plans of several of the Commonwealth fortresses, to Worcester College in Oxford. Clarke Papers, MSxxx f158, (Worcester College, Oxford).
35 Cruden, pp.228–9.
36 Firth, *Scotland and the Protectorate*, p.XL.
37 Dow, p.258.

82   1648 and all that

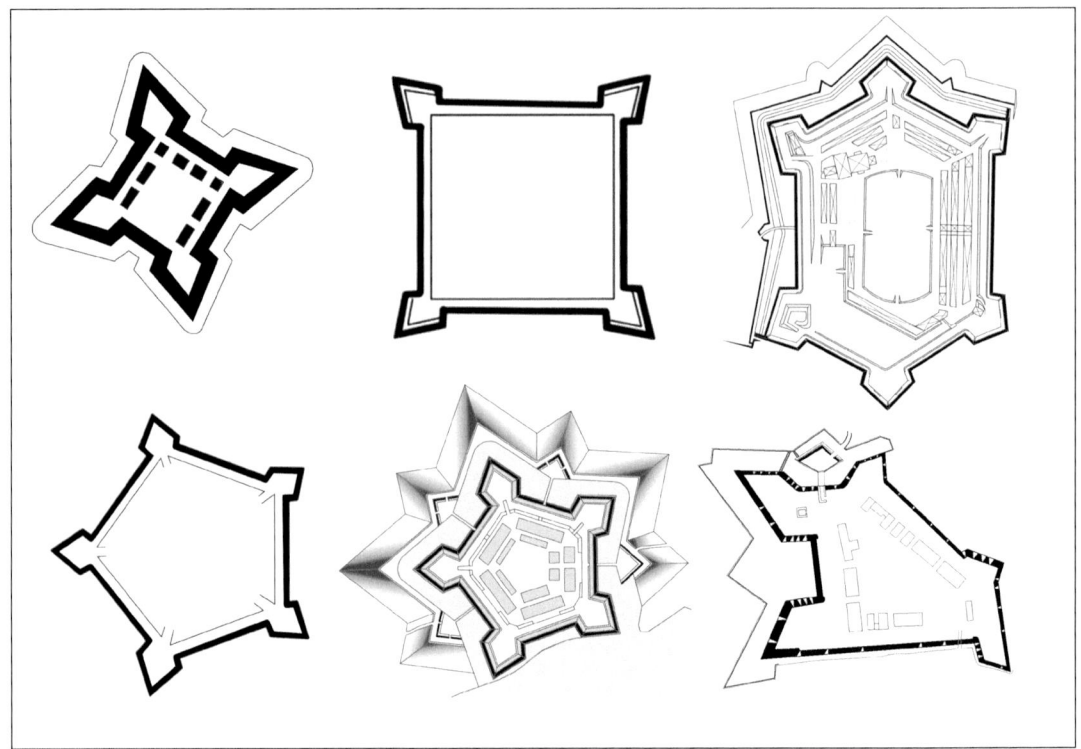

The Protectorate Citadels – Comparison (Top row: Leith (1652), Perth, Ayr. Bottom row: Leith (1656), Inverness, Inverlochy). (Artwork by Charles Blackwood)

Following the restoration, the citadels were a stark reminder of the previous regime, and were expensive to maintain. John Maitland, Earl of Lauderdale, and the most powerful nobleman in Scotland, persuaded Charles II that it would be appropriate to 'raze it [Inverlochy] and the other forts erected in Scotland by that great wicked man'.[38] No longer could the government afford to maintain these symbols of Cromwellian rule, and so instruction was given to slight the forts and disperse the garrisons.

Yet two years later, in 1662, two regiments of foot and a troop of horse, based at Leith under Morgan's command, still remained to be disbanded (there was the little matter of arrears of pay, totalling £30,000), and it wasn't until May that it could be reported that 'all the citidaillis quhairin the English sodgeries wer quarterit wer now emptied [all the citadels wherein the English soldiers were quartered were now emptied]', their occupants paid off or shipped from Leith to Lisbon or Tangier, and thus, the military occupation of Scotland ended, 'and their wes none in airmes in all Scotland, ather native or stranger, except the leiff gaird for this Majesteis use and weill of his subjects'.[39]

With the citadels now empty, attention could be given to their disposal: 'Discharge by James Stansfield, burgess in Edinburgh, in favour of Patrick Threapland, merchant in Perth, on behalf of the

38   Quoted in Tabraham and Grove, p.19.
39   Sir Charles Firth and Godfrey Davies, *The Regimental History of Cromwell's Army*, (Oxford: Oxford University Press, 1940), volume II, pp.498–9, John Nicoll, *A Diary of Public Transactions*, (Edinburgh: Bannatyne Club, 1836), p.367, and Dow, p.276.

magistrates, council and inhabitants thereof, for £366 13s 4d sterling as the just proportion which the King had appointed the 'donator' of Perth citadel to pay for the satisfaction of the English workmen concerned in the building of Leith citadel'.[40]

Leith citadel was given to Lauderdale, who promptly persuaded (some say blackmailed!) Edinburgh to buy it back from him and within 10 years it was mostly disused and partially demolished.

With the citadels abandoned, the garrisons returned to the Royal castles. But despite existing for less than a decade, the citadels provided a valuable lesson: namely their placement enabled them to defend strategic locations, and command surrounding lands. This lesson would be learnt by a generation of engineers and tacticians and would dominate military engineering in Scotland for the next century. But whilst these new citadels represented the shape of things to come, they did not quite mean the end of the castle. The Restoration government's preference for the existing medieval castle over the modern citadel, the cost of upkeep notwithstanding, suggests that perhaps the citadels were not quite the finished article, or perhaps more likely, part of the general amnesia towards anything connected with the interregnum.

Regardless of the cost of constructing and maintaining the citadels, they taught an important lesson to both the government and a generation of military engineers, something highlighted by Monck who wrote that the citadel at Inverlochy was 'a great deale of benefit to your Highness, besides the securitie of the place and the advantage wee may have by laying fewer men there, if any troubles should be'.[41] Considering that the Protectorate government maintained a force of 10,000 soldiers to police Scotland, the size of the army which existed for most of the reign of Charles II rarely more than 2,000 strong, was totally inadequate, even more so considering that this force would also garrison the Royal castles and other strong points, as well as defending Scotland from external threat.

During the reign of Charles II, the chief garrisons were the Royal castles: Edinburgh, Stirling, and Dumbarton, as well as Blackness. Each castle had a small permanent staff: a governor, other officers, gunners, soldiers (which would be supplemented by companies from the regiments of guards), and sometimes miners. Supporting this would be gunsmiths, wheelwrights, carpenters, and so on, as well as storekeepers. As the headquarters of the Scottish command, Edinburgh Castle was also home to the Major General of the Scottish forces, the Physician General, and the Adjutant General.

To the government, the biggest threat to the internal security of Scotland were the Highland clans, and their control was the overriding priority for Scottish military planning for the next 100 years. The slighting of the citadels at Inverness and Inverlochy had removed any government garrisons from the Highlands, and given the pitiful size of the army in Scotland, for much of Charles' reign it was felt that the Highlands were too great a risk to even contemplate.[42]

As a consequence, there were constant calls to reinstate a garrison at Inverlochy: in 1664, 40 foot-guards were stationed in the Inverlochy area, 'the chiefs in the neighbourhood being charged to provide these troops with fire and bedding'. The soldiers were stationed there to preserve the peace against 'herships, theiftes, robers and depredations daylie commited upon His Majesties peacable and obedient subjects'.[43] But this force was far too tiny to have any impact, and the strategy of attempting to solve the issue from within, by issuing commissions to the Earl of Atholl in 1667, and Sir James Campbell of Lawers, and Colonel James Menzies in 1678 for 'securing the peace of the Highlands' proved to be

---

40 Perth & Kinross Council Archive, *Military affairs*, B59/32/2.
41 General George Monck, quoted in Tabraham and Grove, p.19.
42 Tabraham and Grove, p.26.
43 Quoted in Tabraham and Grove, p.26.

84   1648 and all that

equally unsuccessful. But despite the internal threat to the peace and security of the kingdom, it was the threat from the Dutch which prompted the construction of the only new fortress to be built in Scotland during the reign of Charles II.

Master Masons to the Crown of Scotland

The Scottish military establishment did not contain a military engineering function, so the task of construction and maintaining the country's fortifications fell to the King's Master Mason, a post occupied for much of the reign of Charles II by Robert Mylne (1633–1710). Mylne was the grandson of John Mylne the elder (d.1657, who was Master Mason to the Crown between 1631 and 1639), and nephew of John Mylne the younger (1611–1667). The younger John Mylne succeeded his father as Master Mason, and, during the English invasion of 1650, had strengthened Edinburgh's walls and constructed artillery emplacements.

Burgh Records note that John Mylne used some of the stonework removed from the Spur at Edinburgh Castle, as part of the overall improvements to the castle's defences, to repair Leith's fortifications.[44] He

The contribution of Robert Mylne to the fortifications of Edinburgh Castle is marked in the name of Mills Mount Battery. The *echaugette* (sentinel turret) was added in c.1735. (David Flintham)

44   M. Wood (ed.), *Extracts from the Records of the Burgh of Edinburgh, 1642–55*, (Edinburgh: Scottish Burgh Records Society, 1938), p.197.

may well have been involved in the construction of a line of earthworks linking Edinburgh to Leith, but following the Scottish defeat, Mylne changed sides and worked for the English, constructing the first fort at Leith.[45]

Robert Mylne was the last Master Mason to the Crown of Scotland, and in this role was responsible for works at the Royals castles, including repairs at Edinburgh Castle in 1662, 1677, and 1685. There is a record of Mylne rebuilding the 'foir bastner' in 1662, which is likely to have been the Cromwellian hornwork.[46]

There is a battery on the north side of Edinburgh Castle called 'Mills Mount' which was named in connection with the work undertaken by Mylne. It was the availability of funds and the willingness of the Privy Council rather than any overall strategy which determined where and when these works would take place.

Another Royal appointment was that of the overseer of the Royal works in Scotland, a post held for part of the reign of Charles II by James Smith who, at the age of 70, supervised the construction of the barracks at Inversnaid (close to Loch Lomond) in 1719.[47]

Fort Charlotte

Mylne's most important military work was in the furthest reaches of the Kingdom, in a location so far away it was nearer to Norway than it was Edinburgh. The anchorage in Bressay Sound, Shetland,[48] was an important safe haven for the Royal Navy, although previously, it was a favoured stopping place for ships of the Dutch East India Company who found the north of the British Isles a safer way back to the North Sea rather than facing the British warships in the English Channel. The presence of the Dutch ships was something of a boon to the local Shetland economy.

But with the outbreak of the Second Dutch War in 1665, it was realised that the Dutch might return and thus the Sound needing defending. However, the loyalties of the Shetlanders were also questionable, causing Lord Rothes, who was sent to Lerwick to assess suitable locations for a fort, to comment that the Shetlanders had a 'greater affection to the Dutch than they have either to Scots or to English'.[49] Rothes discovered that the likely sites for a fort in terms of protecting the anchorage were all overlooked by high ground to the landward side. Added to this Rothes felt that the soil was too thin to support the bastions. But eventually, a suitable site was found, and Mylne was instructed to draw up a plan, one that drew heavily on the plans for the earlier Cromwellian fortresses: the plan was for a bastioned fort, roughly pentagonal in shape, and, overlooking the sound, a zig-zag parapet. It could house a garrison of 100 men in a single barrack block.

Its magazine, a 'Cellar call'd powder Room', was outside the fort (presumably to limit the danger of accidental explosion, but presenting an additional risk should the fort ever be attacked), and would later fulfil a different role: 'Lerwick, 20 September 1670 Disposition by Laurence Sinclair, sometime

---

45 R. S. Mylne, *The Master Masons to the Crown of Scotland and their Works* (Edinburgh: Scott, Ferguson and Burness, 1893), p.145.
46 Royal Commission of Ancient and Historical Monuments for Scotland, *An Inventory of the Ancient and Historical Monuments of the City of Edinburgh with the Thirteenth Report of the Commission*, (Edinburgh: HMSO, 1951), p.8.
47 Tabraham and Grove, p.61.
48 Historic Environment Scotland, *Statement of Significance: Fort Charlotte*, (Edinburgh: Historic Environment Scotland, 2014).
49 Tabraham and Grove, p.27.

baillie of Lerwick, to justices of the peace in Yetland, of ammunition house standing in the low battery at Lerwick, to be used as a common prison house'.[50]

In actual fact, the fort was not completed until a century later, and was only then named Fort Charlotte in honour of the Queen of George III.

An account of 1701 by a Mr. Brand observed:

> At the North end of the Town, is the Castle or Citadel, of Lerwick, begun to be built in the time, of the Dutch War Anno 1665, by Work-men sent by Authority from Scotland, for that end, but the Work was never perfected, the Work men, returning home, Anno, 1667. At that time also 300 Souldiers were sent over for the Defence of the Countrey, against the hostile Incursions of the Hollanders, and were quartered in places nigh to the Fort, who likewise returned home about the same time, with the Workmen: The Garrison could do much to command the Sound (for then there was no Town here) so that none durst Land nigh unto them; The walls are yet in a good condition, high in some places without, but filled up with Earth within, whereon they raised their Cannon; the weakest part of the Wall towards the North, there hath been a Sally-port, dangerous to Attack, by reason of a deep Ditch before it, fed by a Spring, into which the Garison by cunning Artifices might endeavour draw the Enemy, who by the Stratagems of War thus being brought on, and ensnared, did incontinent sink down into the Sound below them at the foot the Hill, whereupon the Castle is situated: With the Walls is a House of Guard, which hath been two Stories high, burnt by the Dutch, after that our Souldiers had left the Fort. Upon the Walls towards the Sound, are standing 3 Iron Cannons one a 6 another a 7 and a 3d. a 10 Pounder, not left by these who kept Garrison, but since that time within the 30 Years taken out of the Sea nigh to Whalsey, a Ship of Force there being cast away, about 80 Years before: Which Guns the Inhabitants of Lerwick late mounted upon the Walls of the Castle, whereby they might be in a Capacity to Defend themselves against the French Privateers, who at any time should come up the Sound and Assault them.[51]

According to another description:

> There was a fort built at Lerwick by King Charles the 2ds. order anno 1665, and burnt with the town of Lerwick by the Hollanders anno 1673. It stands at the north end of Lerwick. This garison could doe much to command the Sound. Ther was then no town upon the place, so non durst land nigh unto them. The walls are yett in a good condition, high in some places without, but filled up with earth within, wheron they raised their canon. In the weakest part of the wall towards the north, ther heth been a sally port, dangerous to attack, by reason of a deep ditch before it fed by a spring, into which the garison by cunning artifices might indevour to draw the enimy, who by a strategeme of war [...?] brought in and insnared, did incontinently suck down into the Sound below them at the foot of the hill wherupon the castle is situated. Within the wall is ane house of guard which heth been two stories high, which was burnt by the Dutch after that the souldiers had left the fort.
>
> Now there are standing 3 iron cannons upon the walls towards the Sound, one a 6, another a 7, and a 3d. a 10 pounder, not left by the garison bot since that tyme taken out of the sea nigh to Whalsay, a ship of force that cast away about [90?] years before, which guns the inhabitants of Lerwick lately mounted upon the walls of the castle wherby they might be in a capacity to defend themselves against the French privateers,

---

50 Shetland Archives, GD144/73/1.
51 *Brand's Description of Orkney, Shetland, etc.*, (1701). With thanks to John Ballantyne.

who at any tyme sould come up the Sound and assault them.⁵²

In 1666, the fort's governor, Captain Sinclair, complained to Lauderdale that the smalle Guns and the greatest but demi culverines soe too smalle for the batteries towards the sea or Sound, neither have they balle ffor those they have'.⁵³ But fortunately for Sinclair, Dutch intelligence wasn't particularly outstanding: Admiral Van Ghent, the commander of the fleet of 24 ships sent to capture Shetland in June 1667, understood the garrison to be 1,000 men and 40 guns. By the time of Van Ghent's approach, the fort was largely an earthwork one, strengthened with palisades and stockades, but the masonry had not been progressed, and work was halted in July 1667 when the Treaty of Breda ended the war. By November 1667, the fort had already cost £28,000, and so the order was given to disband the garrison and slight the fortifications, a premature decision as in 1672, during the Third Dutch War (1672–7), the Dutch actually did land, and burnt the abandoned barrack block, as well as some buildings in the town.⁵⁴

Fort Charlotte's South Gate – the original 1660s gate was reduced in size to allow only pedestrian only access when the fort was rebuilt during the 1770s. (Otter [CC BY-SA 3.0 (http://creativecommons.org/licenses/by-sa/3.0/)])

John Slezer

John Slezer (before 1650–1717; probably Dutch, although possibly from Germany) had been trained as a military engineer in the Dutch Army. Not only was he skilled in surveying and in the planning, construction, and maintenance of fortification, he was also a skilled artist. Slezer would later recount

---

52   *Ane Description of Zetland* ..., National Library of Scotland, (Adv. MS. 15.1.5, ff. 22–4).
53   Quoted in Noel Fojut and Denys Pringle, *The ancient monuments of Shetland*, (Edinburgh: HMSO, 1993), pp.56–8.
54   Fojut and Pringle, p.58.

being upon travels in the year 1669, I came to Scotland, where I met with great civilities and especially from the late Earls of Argyll and Kincardine, to whome I had the honour to become particularly known. I had their lordships favour to that degree, that they proposed I should be employed here, but no occasion then offering I left the Kingdom. Three years thereafter I had letters from them most kindly inviting me to embrace a post in the army they had procured for me.[55]

So, towards the end of 1671, Slezer returned to Scotland as the chief engineer. For the first time, the role of military engineer was recognised as being a key part of the Scottish military establishment.

Slezer first drew up plans for the repair and improvement of Edinburgh Castle. Submitted to the Treasurer Depute, Charles Maitland of Hatton, these plans are the earliest accurate survey plans of Scottish fortifications.

In addition, he was also commissioned as Lieutenant of the Artillery Train. His commission provides remarkable insight into how the Scottish artillery was organised:

First, he is to make a trial of his skill in artillery and fireworks at the King's charge before them as soon as he conveniently can and for that end they are to cause to be erected for him a laboratory or working house in Edinburgh Castle.

Secondly, they are to signify to the Earl of Linlithgow and the Governors of the Castles of Edinburgh, Stirling and Dumbarton that the said Slezar choose one man out of each company of the Regiment of Guards. Five out of the garrison of Edinburgh, three out of that of Stirling Castle and two out of that of Dumbarton to instruct and train them in all things belonging to artillery as gunnery, casting hand grenadoes and fireworks, and that the said Slezar shall have full command over those 20 men till they be perfectly instructed and then he is choose others as he shall see cause.

Thirdly, that all the gunners in the forts, garrisons and land forces are to obey the said Slezar as the King's lieutenant of artillery in all things relating to his office.

Fourthly, that all gunners that be here-after placed in forts, garrisons and land forces shell be examined and approved by the said Slezar.

Fifthly, that he signify to them what gunners to them what gunners, cannons, mortar pieces, grenades and all other instruments and materials of artillery he shall think fit to transport from one place or garrison to another, and that they give him their warrant for their transportation and particularly what great brass guns he shall think fit to transport from Dumbarton Castle.

Sixthly, that he make an inventory of all guns and other materials belonging to the artillery and signify to them what carriages or other necessary things are wanting.

Seventhly, that he provide all things which the King shall think fit hereafter to be added to the artillery and they give hime their warrant for it from time to time, he being always accountable to them in every thing.

Eighthly, that he shall visit all castles and garrisons at least twice a year, and report to them of his diligence for which end they are to give order that he be provided with convenient lodging in all the forts and castles.[56]

Slezer's career was remarkable and unique. In 1678, he was made a burgess of Dundee, and 10 years later, he was promoted to Captain of the Artillery Train. For 46 years he oversaw Scotland's fortresses,

---

55   Quoted in Tabraham and Grove, pp.29–30.
56   John Slezer's warrant as Lieutenant of the Artillery Train (1671). Reproduced in Tabraham and Grove, pp.30–31.

and during this time he supervised building works at all the Royal garrisons. Whilst much of his works were replaced during the Jacobite Rebellions of the following century, a considerable amount remains to this day. Both Blackness and Dumbarton Castles[57] retain their respective Spur batteries, covering their entrances. But Slezer's best remaining works are those in Edinburgh Castle, where his perimeter wall which is wrapped around the Upper Ward, and is loopholed for muskets and light artillery. This perimeter is pierced by Foog's Gate, and in 1681, the now famous medieval bombard, *Mons Meg*, was dumped there.[58]

Not only did he bring improvements to Scotland's fortifications, he also oversaw the transformation of military engineering in Scotland: in 1671, his appointment was a personal one, but by the time of his death in 1717, it was an established department comprising of a chief engineer, an engineer and normally two assistant engineers. This was part of the overall expansion of the Board of Ordnance in Britain. In 1683, the board was restructured and its functions defined in its *Rule Orders and Instructions*. In 1699, the board comprised of 10 engineers (of which the Scottish establishment was part of), and increased to 29 in 1745 (with at least six in Scotland).[59] He also transformed the Artillery Train, establishing a hierarchy of gunners, practitioner gunners, bombardiers, petardiers and miners. He also introduced a system of training for gunners.

Following the deposition of James VII/II, Slezer fought against the forces of William III, but at the end of the Jacobite Rising of 1689, Slezer was imprisoned, but was released the following year, after declaring an oath of fidelity to William III, which procured him a commission as 'captain of the Artillery Company and Surveyor of Magazines'.[60] Five years later, he published the first volume of the work for which today, Slezer is best known: *Theatrum Scotiae containing the prospects of their majesties Castles and Palaces Towns and Colleges the ruins of many ancient Abbeys, Churches, Monasteries and Convents within the said Kingdom all curiously engraven on copper plates with a short description of each place*

Blackness Castle from the south. John Slezer's improvements focused mostly on the western (left-hand) end. (Michael and Lilian Cockburn)

57 Historic Environment Scotland, *Statement of Significance: Blackness Castle*, (Edinburgh: Historic Environment Scotland, 2013), and Historic Environment Scotland, *Statement of Significance: Dumbarton Castle*, (Edinburgh: Historic Environment Scotland, 2015).
58 Historic Environment Scotland, *Statement of Significance: Edinburgh Castle*, (Edinburgh: Historic Environment Scotland, 2012).
59 Carolyn Anderson and Christopher Fleet, *Scotland – Defending the Nation*, (Edinburgh: Birlinn Limited, 2018), p.52.
60 Carolyn J. Anderson, 'Military Intelligence: The Board of Ordnance Maps and Plans of Scotland, 1689–c.1760', in Gary A. Boyd and Denis Linehan (ed.), *Ordnance: War and Architecture & Space*, (Farnha: Ashgate Publishing Limited, 2013), p.175, fn 3.

by John Slezer, Captain of the Artillery Company, and Surveyor of Their Majesties Stores and Magazines in the Kingdom of Scotland.

Slezer's engravings were noted for their accuracy. The *Theatrum* includes some of the first representations of many parts of Scotland, as well as images of buildings that no longer survive. Thus, it is an indispensable source for Scotland's history. Although Slezer could travel around the country at the Government's expense, *Theatrum Scotiae* never repaid its production costs, and the cumulative effects of this and the Government not paying its debts (Slezer had to pay the costs for clothing the artillery company out of his own pocket), left Slezer bankrupt. Whilst he did not keep his accounts in good order, his testament describes him as an 'indweller in the Abbay of Holyroodhouse' (the confines of the old Abbey were used to provide debtors protection from their creditors).[61]

John Slezer's design for the eastern defences of Edinburgh Castle are visible in *Plattegrond van het kasteel van Edinburgh*, 1692, Samuel Du Ry de Champdoré. (Rijksmuseum, Amsterdam)

The (not so) Glorious Revolution

In November 1688, William of Orange disposed his father-in-law, James VII/II, but it was not until the following March that the Scottish Parliament debated the succession to the Scottish crown. The so called 'Convention Parliament' was equally divided between the supporters of James (the 'Jacobites') and the supporters of William (the 'Williamites'), but when, on 4 April 1689, it was decided to offer

---

61   *Testament of John Slezer*, National Records of Scotland, CC8/8/87, p.159.

the crown to William, Jacobitism was born. The predominate Catholic and Episcopalian clans in the Highlands now had a common cause (in addition of course, to their undying hatred of Clan Campbell). But even before the final decision had been reached, the leader of the Jacobites, John Graham of Claverhouse, Viscount Dundee, had quit Parliament to raise support across the country. On 18 March, Dundee scaled the western side of the Castle Rock, and met with the governor of Edinburgh Castle, the Duke of Gordon who, being a devout Catholic pledged to hold the castle 'for the King, though the Prince of Orange should obtain possession of every other fortress in the Kingdom'.[62]

Yet Edinburgh Castle was garrisoned by just 120 men, and had 100 barrels of gunpowder for its 22 cannons. The garrison was thus outnumbered by the 800 men of the Earl of Leven's Regiment which arrived first before the castle, and even more so by the three Williamite regiments (Balfour's, Mackay's, and Romsey's), commanded by Major General Hugh Mackay of Scourie, which replaced Leven's soon afterwards. Whilst Mackay initially lacked the heavy artillery necessary to make any impact upon the fabric of the castle, the garrison lacked the numbers to make sorties, nor would the garrison fire on the city of Edinburgh itself. But in April, the arrival of mortars enabled Mackay to bombard the castle, forcing the garrison to take shelter beneath the Half-Moon battery.[63] Finally, on 13 June Gordon surrendered.[64] On the 27th of the following month, Mackay was defeated by Dundee at the Battle of Killiecrankie, but the death of Dundee at the moment of victory, and the defeat of the Jacobites at Dunkeld on 21 August bought the 1689 rebellion to an end. For Scotland, at least, the so called 'Glorious Revolution' was anything but glorious.

The following year, with growing unrest in Ireland and the possibility of renewed Jacobite activity in Scotland, Sir Martin Beckman, Chief Engineer to the Office of Ordnance advised that 'no Monarch, Prince or State has been, nor can be, safe in their government without tenable fortifications for the magazines and security for their respective seaports'.[65]

Fort William

The fact that most of Dundee's army at Killiecrankie had been recruited from the Catholic and Episcopalian clans around Lochaber (the region at the southern end of the Great Glen) led the Government to recognise that the Western Highlands were 'a good cradle for a rising'.[66] As mentioned previously, since the slighting of the Cromwellian fort, there had been numerous calls for the re-establishment of a garrison at Inverlochy: John Slezer commented that the Cromwellian fort had 'contributed much to keep the Highlands in Subjection to the Government, and in an intire Peace amongst themselves'.[67] But whether it was due to indifference or lack of money (or a combination of both), these calls were ignored.

Following the outbreak of rebellion in the summer of 1689, the Convention Parliament when went as far as passing a resolution to fortify Inverlochy, but it was not until 1 March 1690, with a deterioration in the situation in Ireland, together with the spectre of the western clans united in rebellion, that Mackay was given the necessary resources. In July, at the head of 7,000 troops, Mackay met a small

---

62 Andrew Murray Scott, *Bonnie Dundee*, (Edinburgh: John Donald, 2000), p.101; Tabraham and Grove, p.35.
63 An archaeological excavation in this area in 1986 uncovered the skeletons of 15 young men. See Tabraham and Grove, pp.38–9.
64 W, Forbes Gray, *A Short History of Edinburgh Castle*, (Edinburgh: Moray Press, 1948), pp.59–63.
65 Sir Martin Beckman, quoted in Anderson, 'Military Intelligence …' p.166.
66 Quoted in Tabraham and Grove, p.39.
67 John Slezer, quoted in Anderson, 'Military Intelligence …' p.166.

fleet of ships by Loch Linnhe and construction commenced. But he was unable to plan an entirely new fort – constrained by topography and limited resources, Mackay was forced to reuse the Cromwellian structure, noting 'the situation of the old fort did not please me, being commanded from a near hill, but I could not change it, there being none else to fit'.[68] However, the site utilised the natural defensive position on the angle of land where the River Nevis flows into Loch Linnhe (thus enabling the fort to be supplied by sea).

The new fort took around a fortnight to construct, and by the time Mackay left for Stirling, he was able to report 'in 11 days I got it at its full height, the matter of 20 feet from the bottom of the fosse, palisaded round with a *chemin couvert* [covered way] and glacis, a perfect defence'[69]. He departed 'leaving 1,000 men in garrison in the new built fort'.[70] Given the time it took to construct the new fort, it is of no surprise that what was constructed amounted to a simple palisaded earthwork. As well as the garrison of 1,000, it was armed with fifteen 12-pounder cannon, removed from the ships.

The remains of Fort William today (the sally port /sea gate dates from the original Cromwellian Inverlochy fort). (David Flintham)

68 Major General Hugh Mackay, *Memoirs of the War carried on in Scotland and Ireland*, 1689–91, (Edinburgh: The Bannatyne Club, 1833), p.98.
69 Mackay, pp.98–9.
70 Mackay, p.99.

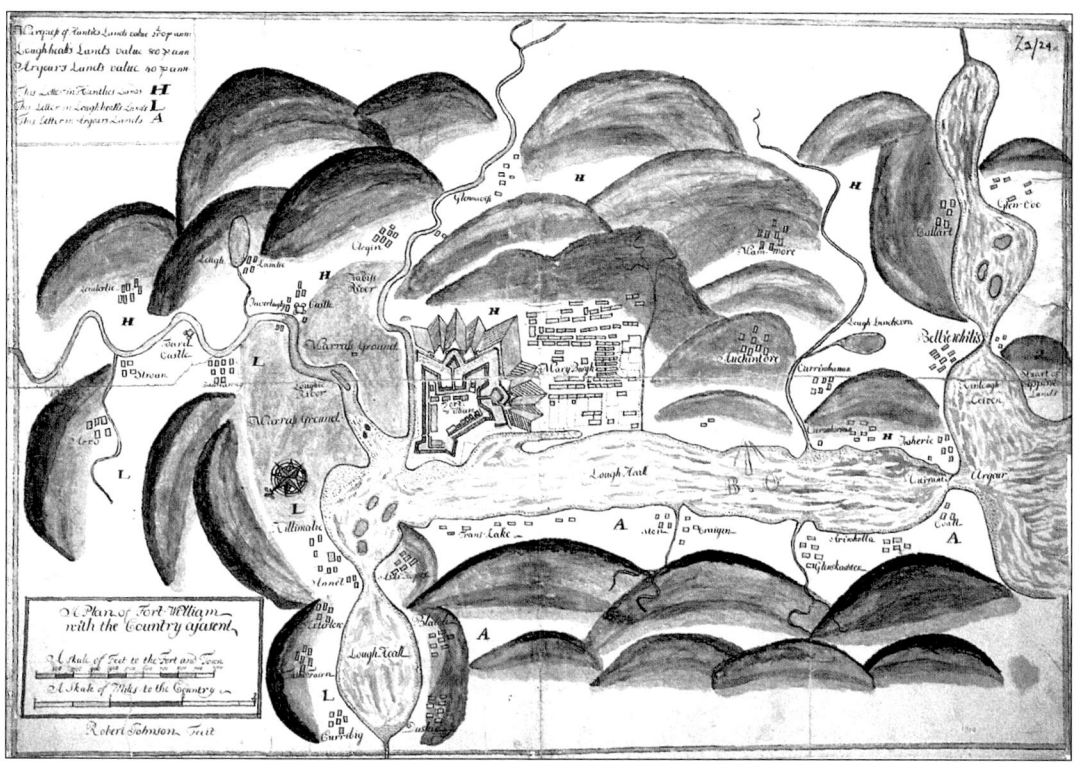

Plan of Fort William with the country adjacent (Robert Johnson c.1710). (Reproduced with the permission of the National Library of Scotland)

Despite early desertions and a mutiny later in 1690, the fort gradually gained permanence, especially when, towards the end of the decade, stone walls, up to 6.1 metres (20 feet) in height, replaced the original earthworks. The north-eastern wall of this irregular-shaped fort abutted the River Ness and was protected by a demi-bastion. Along this wall there was also a sally-port, likely to have been left over from the original Cromwellian fort. The north-west face, overlooking marshy ground, was protected by a demi-bastion. To the south, landward sides were protected by two further bastions, and fronted by a ditch. The southern and eastern sides were additionally protected by a riveted glacis, and a ravelin guarded the entrance to the fort. The fort was demolished to make way for the coming of the railway in the nineteenth century. The remains of the fort visible today show the two building periods, with the earlier 1650s construction comprising of large river boulders. The sea-gate/ sally port dates from the 1650s and is shown on the plan of 1656.

Yet even the strengthened reconstruction was viewed as inadequate by some; in 1710, the engineer Talbot Edwards reported 'This Forte for defending it self is indeed but a ill figure'.[71] Yet despite this, and the fact that it stood at the foot of a mountain and was thus within musket shot, it was the only garrisoned fort to withstand a siege by the Jacobites during the 1645 Rebellion.

71 Talbot Edwards, quoted in Anderson, 'Military Intelligence …', p.166.

Named 'Fort William' in honour of King William III (the Gaelic name for Fort William, *An Gearasdan*, translates as 'The Garrison'), the fort's first governor was Colonel John Hill, who had also served at the original Cromwellian fort. The role of the garrison was to police the Western Highlands, and soldiers were out-posted to minor garrisons across the region. However, the garrison of Fort William would also be involved in the massacre in Glencoe in the early hours of 13 February 1692. The garrison became a permanent one, and soon after the fort was completed, Hill received a Royal charter for the creation of a neighbouring civilian settlement, which was named 'Maryburgh', after Queen Mary.

Kilchurn Castle

47 km to the south of Fort William, standing on the shores of Loch Awe at the western end of Glen Orchy, stands Kilchurn Castle. A picturesque ruin today, this late-medieval castle was at the heart of the political intrigue which characterised later seventeenth century Scotland.

The turbulent decline and subsequent dismemberment of the once mighty Clan MacDonald empire during the fifteenth century created a void in the Western Highlands of Scotland, one which Clan Campbell was only too willing to fill. It was, therefore, at the expense of the MacDonalds that the Campbells acquired their immense wealth and power. Centred upon Argyllshire, the Campbells came

Kilchurn Castle – the 1690s barrack block is on the left. (Alex Flintham)

to dominate the southern regions of the Western Highlands, consolidating their position through the construction of several castles including those at Inveraray and Kilchurn.

Kilchurn Castle even today is in a secluded location, yet when construction commenced in the 1450s, it was even more isolated as it was originally situated on an island, connected to the shore by an underwater causeway (today, there is easy land access to Kilchurn Castle as a result of the lowering of the level of the loch during the nineteenth century). The castle was initially constructed as a five-storey, battlemented tower house for Sir Colin Campbell, first Lord of Glenorchy. By the middle of the sixteenth century, the castle had been remodelled with the addition of a range and a hall to its southern side. During the seventeenth century, Kilchurn Castle was at the centre of a clan dispute with the MacGregors and later, in 1654, the castle was besieged, but neither incident caused significant (or any) damage to the castle.[72]

Born about 1635, John Campbell of Glenorchy was created the first Earl of Breadalbane in 1681. Following the succession of William and Mary, Breadalbane (who was reputed to own the best wig in Scotland!) commenced a dangerous political game, seeming to support both the Government and the Jacobites – to some he was William's 'man of business', but to others he was 'a known enemy of their Majesty's service'.[73] What is clear, however, that Breadalbane principally supported one cause – his own, and his ambition to make himself the undisputed master of the entire region.

In the mid-1680s, Breadalbane had unsuccessfully proposed the formation of a Highland militia, under his command naturally, to police the Highlands. By 1689, his designs for a Government-sponsored 'private army' hadn't gone away but this time, his strategy was different. He would convert his principle residence of Kilchurn Castle into a fortified barracks. It was already a place of strength, described as 'ane real stronghold', 'invirond on tuo sids with deep rivers, and a ditch and trench befor it'.[74]

Breadalbane was determined that his re-modelled castle would rival Fort William, and despite financial difficulties, work commenced in late 1690 and continued through to 1698. The re-modelling of Kilchurn was intended to provide accommodation for three companies of soldiers and officers, some 200 men. The resulting L-shaped barrack block is probably the oldest surviving example in mainland Britain.[75]

But it is not clear exactly how the refurbished accommodation was to be used. It is likely that it was no longer intended to be Breadalbane's principle residence, and his private lodging would be converted for use by officers. A new three-story L-shaped barrack block was constructed along the north/ north-eastern range of the castle. Each floor would accommodate a company, and was divided into four rooms. Kitchens and latrines were also provided. It is likely that the north-eastern block accommodated NCOs. Additional accommodation was provided in the attic space and in the upper-floors of the existing projecting round towers. In 1693, the great door-lintel bearing his arms and the initials of himself and of his wife was put in place.

The last year for which there are building accounts of Kilchurn Castle is 1698 (coincidentally, the same year in which work commenced on the re-building of Fort William in stone). So, it is safe to assume that the building work ceased then, before any external bastions and other defensive works

---

72 David Flintham, 'A Campbell's Kingdom – Kilchurn Castle', *Casemate*, number 98, (Fortress Study Group, 2013), pp.43–44, 55.
73 Tabraham and Grove, p.42.
74 Tabraham and Grove, p.42.
75 Historic Environment Scotland, *Statement of Significance: Kilchurn Castle*, (Edinburgh: Historic Environment Scotland, 2004).

could be constructed. Breadalbane had run out of money. He lived to see the irony of Kilchurn being garrisoned by Government troops during the 1715 rising (typically, Breadalbane attempted to support both sides – it was only his death on 19 March 1717, that prevented an inquiry into his conduct).

Theodore Dury and the Act of Union

John Slezer's successor as engineer was another émigré, Theodore Dury (1661–1742). Dury was a Huguenot and fled France following the revocation of the Edict of Nantes in 1685.[76] He was first recorded as an artilleryman serving with the Williamite forces which besieged Edinburgh Castle in 1689, and four years later, he joined Slezer's team of engineers. From February 1693, Dury was employed as the chief military engineer in Scotland,[77] and was responsible for state fortifications in Scotland including a new fort at Inverness in 1690,[78] which was constructed on a new site (the Cromwellian citadel was demolished in 1661 and never rebuilt), on the Castle Hill. Built on the orders of General Mackay, whilst it had modern ramparts and demi-bastions, it did embody an older tower-house and a system of irregular curtain walls which were likely to have been mediaeval in origin.[79]

Dury married Mary Ann Bowlier, and had a daughter, Olympia, who was baptised on 29 January 1701 in Edinburgh. On 25 August 1702, he was commissioned as chief engineer in Scotland by Queen Anne,[80] who had succeeded her brother-in-law, William, less than six months before, and on 25 March 1707 he was naturalised as a Scot.[81] He would go on to propose ambitious programmes of works for both Edinburgh and Stirling Castles, with Dury's and Butt's Batteries, and the Queen Anne Building at the former,[82] and the outer defences covering the entrance at the latter[83] all remaining to this day. Dury was also involved in improvements to Fort William, particularly the garrison buildings.

Two years after Dury's commission, a new succession crisis saw the passing of the 1704 Act of Security which declared that, in the event of Queen Anne's death, Scotland might opt for a different monarch from that agreed for England. As a result, the flame of Jacobitism flickered into life again, and burst into flames when the 1707 Act of Union between Scotland and England was passed. The Act of Union also brought the army in Scotland under the control of the Board of Ordnance.

Whilst an actual uprising the year after the Act of Union was aborted, the fact that the rising had the support of Louis XIV threatened a completely new dimension to the War of Spanish Succession, and as such, was a threat that could not be ignored. It prompted the Government in London to look again at the security of what was now called 'North Britain' and led to the next phase of fortress construction in Scotland.

---

76   D. Dobson, *Huguenot and Scots Links 1575–1775*, (Baltimore: Clearfield, 2005), p.5.
77   National Archive of Scotland, GD124/13/49.
78   National Archive of Scotland, GD26/9/111; National Archive MPHH 1/38.
79   Cruden, p. 241.
80   National Archive of Scotland, GD124/13/49; R. P. Mahaffy (editor), *Calendar of State Papers, Domestic Series: Queen Anne*, (London: Public Record Office, 1916), volume I, p.496.
81   Gordon Ewart and Dennis Gallagher, *Fortress of the Kingdom: Archaeology and Research at Edinburgh Castle*, (Edinburgh: Historic Scotland, 2014), p.112.
82   Historic Environment Scotland, *Statement of Significance: Edinburgh Castle – Queen Anne Building*, (Edinburgh: Historic Environment Scotland, 2012).
83   Historic Environment Scotland, *Statement of Significance: Stirling Castle*, (Edinburgh: Historic Environment Scotland, 2004).

Gezicht op Stirling Castle, Robert Sayer, after Paul Sandby, 1753 featuring Theodore Dury's eastern defences at Stirling Castle. (Rijksmuseum, Amsterdam)

Conclusion

The 50 years following the Act of Union saw existing fortresses improved, and new ones established. The adaptation of Kilchurn Castle into a barracks at virtually the same time as Fort William was being constructed exemplifies the two contrasting theories of fortress design: the fortified barracks, and the garrisoned fort. These two differing models dominated fortress strategy in the Highlands throughout much of the eighteenth century, with Inversnaid and Ruthven typifying the first model, and Fort Augustus the second.

Ruthven is the most well-known of all the fortified barracks built in the Highlands during the eighteenth century, although it owes its origins to a *Report of the Committee anent this peace off the Highlands*, dated 6th December 1699 which said 'It is the opinion of the Committee that a garrison be established at Ruthben of Badenoch consisting at least of thirty sentinels with a Captain and Subalterns, two Sergeants, two Corporals and a Drum'.[84]

Ruthven Barracks was not however built until two decades later.

In my lecture at the 2018 *Century of the Soldier* conference, I considered European influences on fortress warfare during the British Civil Wars. Although by the end of the wars there were more 'home grown' 'engineers' than there were at the outbreak of the fighting, as I have demonstrated here, throughout the second half of the seventeenth century, foreign engineers continued to dominate fortress design and construction, not only in Scotland, but in England as well. The designs of the Cromwellian citadels were reliant on foreign expertise, so, despite a decade of civil war, foreign expertise was at the forefront of military engineering in Britain). The importance of foreign engineers lasted into the eighteenth century: Theodore Dury was succeeded in 1715 as Chief Engineer in Scotland by another French Huguenot, Lewis Petit.

Influence of foreign engineers (Table)

Name	Lived	Nationality	Known for
Richard Deane	1610–1653	English	Perth citadel
John Rosworm	1630–1660	German	Inverness citadel
John Mylne	1611–67	Scottish	First Leith citadel
Hans Ewald Tessin	Died after 1683	Swede or German	Ayr citadel
Robert Mylne	1633–1710	Scottish	Edinburgh Castle, Fort Charlotte
John Slezer	Before 1650–1717	Dutch or German	Blackness, Dumbarton, and Edinburgh Castles
Theodore Dury	1661–1742	French Huguenot	Edinburgh and Stirling Castles, Inverness fort and Fort William

The first half of the eighteenth century witnessed an acceleration in military engineering, with forts, fortified barracks, and military roads being built throughout much of the Highlands, culminating with the construction of Fort George, which in itself represents the ultimate successor to Ayr Citadel, built nearly 100 years before. But arguably the greatest legacy of a century of military engineering is the systematic mapping of Great Britain which traces its origins to the aftermath of the Jacobite Rebellion of 1745–6 when King George II charged Lieutenant Colonel David Watson to undertake a military survey of the Scottish Highlands. He was assisted by William Roy, who would be credited as the father of the Ordnance Survey.

---

84 W. J. Allardyce, *Historical Papers relating to the Jacobite Period, 1699–1750*, (Aberdeen: 1896), volume 1, p.1.

Fort George, constructed in the aftermath of the Battle of Culloden in 1746 is the zenith of Scottish fortress design. But similarities with Ayr Citadel, constructed a century before, are obvious. (David Flintham)

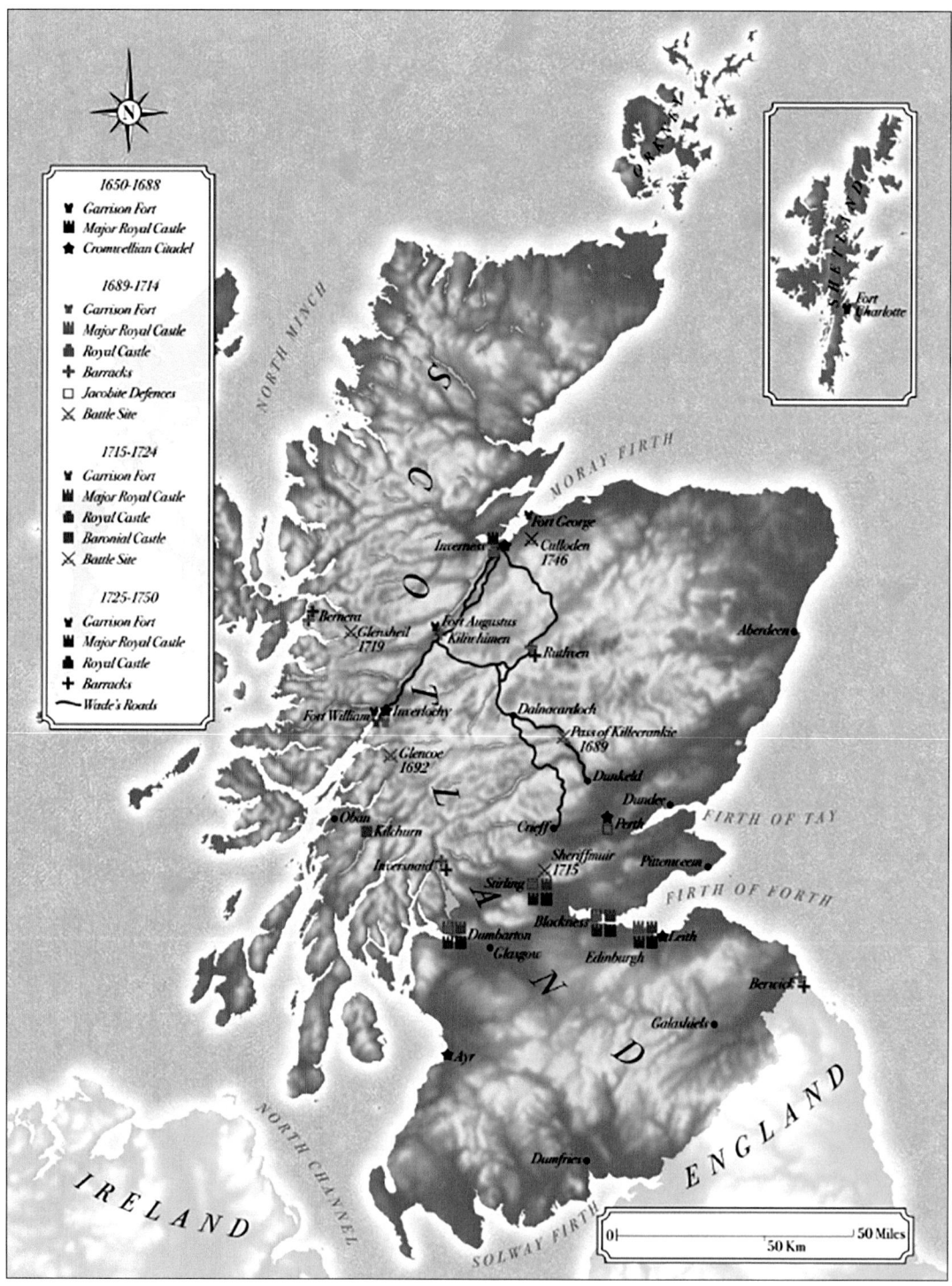

Fortress Scotland, 1650–1750. (Ian Bull (*Military History Matters*))

Logistics of Rebellion 1685 from the 2019 National Army Museum conference

Stephen Carter

A study of logistics needed to turn a 'rabble' into a seventeenth century 'modelled' army

There are many romantic myths that surround the Duke of Monmouth and the Rebellion of 1685, but the most common of these is that he commanded a 'pitchfork army.' It is this popular view that is reinforced by modern writers who regularly portray the rebel forces as 'poorly armed with matchlock muskets and scythes on eight-foot poles … and its men were mostly untrained amateurs'[1] or simply 'weavers and labourers with makeshift weapons.'[2] This has come down from the Victorian historians happy to follow in the footsteps of earlier Jacobite authors who had no interest in portraying Monmouth in a positive light. This idealistic view has also been adopted by modern supporters of Monmouth and is used as an example of the heroic but vanquished underdog, the poor rebel. To support this perspective, there is an often quoted contemporary source which describes the Whigs as 'the Rabble at Frome … between 2 and 3000 were gather together … some with Pistols, some with Pikes and some with Pitch-Forks and Sythes.'[3] This was an article published in the London Gazette on 29 June 1685, and at face value this reinforces the myth. However, if you look below the historical surface, this is not a description of Monmouth's Army but a depiction of the local men gathering at Frome on 25 June 1685. They had come together on the news of Monmouth's approach, and eagerly awaited the arrival of the protestant Duke. Therefore, this is not Monmouth's Army, but a group of supporters with whatever equipment they could find.

The other evidence point that is used to support the 'pitchfork army' myth, is the conversion of scythes into military weapons at Taunton. This order was made after the army was re-modelled into the five regiments, and the council elected to attach a mixed scythe company to each battalion. It is possible that the Lyme Company was formed at the same time, and may have been a large scythe only company which acted as Monmouth's Guards. On 20 June Monmouth's paymaster Captain Thompson wrote the following order for the collection of Scythe blades:

---

1 Saul David, 'All the Kings Men' (London: Penguin Books, 2012), p.3.
2 Anna Keay, *'The Last Royal Rebel'*, (London: Bloomsbury, 2016), p.361.
3 London Gazette #2046, June 26–29, 1685.

102 1648 and all that

Contemporary image of ragged soldiers from the seventeenth century. Authors collection

James R.

These are, in his Majesty's name, to will and require you, on sight hereof, to search for, seize, and take all such scythes as can be found in your tything, paying a reasonable price for the same, and bring them to my house to-morrow by one of the clock in the afternoon, that they may be delivered in to the commission officers that are appointed to receive them at Taunton by four of the same day, and you shall be reimbursed by me what the scythes are worth. And hereof fail not, as you will answer the contrary. Given under my hand this 20th day of June, in the first year of his Majesty's reign.

To the Tything-men of Ch.'[4]

4   George Roberts, *Life, Progresses and Rebellion of James, Duke of Monmouth*, Vol.I, (London: Longmans, 1844) p.328.

This letter was written hours after Monmouth had been proclaimed King and outlines the specific nature of the need for scythes. This is not a general demand for farm implements but for an item that can quickly be turned into a weapon. Which was not a random act as Major Wade writes 'Capt. Richard Slapes company of Scythes & Musketeers being 100 which were added to the Duke's Regiment.' In 1686, King James II wrote that Monmouth's Army had 'five great battalins each of wch had one comp: of at least 100 sythmen, in stead of Grenadeers.' At the Battle of Sedgemoor, some of these 'grenadier' companies appear to have been brigaded into a single battalion under Colonel Brandt, Count of Horne. To support this there is an account written by an eyewitness that 'Munmouth ranged both his horse, and foot forces, and put them in order; Himself, and Count Horn, commanded the Infantry; Count Horn commanded the Sithmen particular, and the Left Wing; Munmouth commanded his maine Batatalia of Foot, and the Lord Greay, commanded the Body of the Calvary.'[5] There is no doubt that by the time Monmouth modelled his army at Taunton, most of the regimented equipment had run out. This had forced the quartermaster and paymaster to look at new options. However, these needed to fit within the existing organisation and not disrupt the fabric of the units.

It is rather unfortunate that the repetitive narrative of the mythical 'pitchfork army' is so well established that in this case it has created a historic blindness. If this order is examined, and cross checked with Wade's narrative and even James II's account, this is explicitly for scythes. This is not a demand for any old farm implement, but for half-pikes to create mixed shot units to act as grenadiers. Another overlooked facet of the order is that it is issued by the paymaster and the army was prepared to pay a bounty for each weapon, another sign this was more than a thrown together rabble.

However, the pitchfork myth is easy to maintain, especially as this is such a well establish view of the campaign. Then there is a different account from the Earl of Clarendon. This paints a very similar picture, as the Earl states that there were only 800 muskets, 500 pairs of pistol and 200 swords landed, and goes on to explain that 'the foot, (all but three or four hundred who marched without any weapon but a cudgel,) were armed with

A stand of Scythes from Roberts publish in 1847. Authors collection

5   National Library of Jamaica, MS 105, 87–8; Supplementary Material, p 13.

muskets, and bags for their powder, and pikes; but in the whole body there was not one pikeman had a corslet, and very few musketeer who had swords'.[6] Undoubtedly, a poorly armed force, but this does not portray Monmouth's Army of 1685, it is a description of King Charles I's Army at Edgehill in 1642.[7] It is interesting that historians do not describe the Royalists as a rabble, as there is a general acceptance that this was the start of a conflict. There is an understanding that armies evolve and develop as supply chains are established. Although, as we will see, Monmouth landed with more arms than his grandfather and had a larger army within the first three weeks of campaigning.

It is a shame for history that the 'pitchfork army' is so entrenched in the popular mind because just below the surface there are detailed spy reports which tell the true story. These contemporary accounts can be found in the British Library and have been totally ignored. However, they give a more accurate and dynamic description of the Whig armies and show that there was little to divide Monmouth at Sedgemoor from his grandfather's army at Edgehill. Excitingly, these secret reports go on to provide other evidence that explain how seventeenth century commanders transformed raw recruits into a fledgling army. By understanding how the Whig armies of 1685 were formed and supplied, a better sense of the logistics behind the rebellion comes into focus. More importantly, the study of general military history gains a unique demonstration of the activities needed to model an army from scratch during this period.

When the eye is cast over this intelligence coming from agents within the Whig ranks, a true picture of the Whigs logistics and planning can be seen. Therefore, even before the invasion fleets sail, within the government circles they speak of a 'Holy War',[8] and 'a very considerable quantity of powder and amunition.'[9] Such was the evidence arriving in Edinburgh from Whitehall, that on 28 May, the Earl of Dumbarton wrote to the Marquis of Atholl with a warning, 'we ar of the opinione, that be raison of the good armes he [Argyll] may have that yor Lop : should not hazard rashly anything.'[10] In Whitehall, just days after Argyll sailed from Holland, King James wrote to the Prince of Orange complaining 'that the three ships, laden with arms and ammunition, from Amsterdam' were sailing to Britain.[11] These letters show that in 1685, the Whigs were not seen as a rabble of peasants armed with pitchforks and rusty muskets but a viable threat to the maintenance of power by King James himself.

There are several parallels between the modelling of the Whig armies in 1685 and those of the Royalist in 1642. They start from a corps of veteran officers who are experienced in European warfare. Each royal commander raises a standard, under which the soldiers are enlisted into companies of foot or troops of horse. Then weapons and uniforms are issued, after which the NCO's begin drilling the raw recruits. When enough companies have been created, they are combined, presented with colours, and formed into regiments. While staff officers handled pay and the communications, scouts were out gathering information. However, before any of this activity could happen, a logistics network was needed to bring everything together. Based on intelligence coming from the government agents in Holland, who had uncovered information on the logistics behind the invasions in Scotland and

---

6 Peter Young, *Edgehill 1642*, (Gloucestershire: The Windrush Press, 1995), p.24.
7 It is interesting that although Charles I's Army was raised on August 23, after two months about five percent of the army remains 'unarmed'. This is after the armouries of the Trained Bands and Royalist noblemen had been emptied.
8 British Library (BL), Add MS 41812, f.37.
9 BL, Add MS 41812, f.55.
10 Blair Archives, 29.I (4), f.62.
11 National Archives (NA), SP 8/3, f.131.

England, from the start the Whigs had a far more mature logistics infrastructure than the Royalists did in 1642.

The Whigs state of readiness was due in in part to the planning that had started after Charles II dissolved the Oxford Parliament of 1681. With this act the King also killed the Exclusion Bill, which if passed into law would have made the succession of James, Duke of York illegal. This left the Whigs with no other option but to plan for an uprising when the catholic James was crowned. This level of readiness is one of the many overlooked aspects of the 1685 campaign, as is the desire to be more than a rabble. This become clear even very early in the planning, when in 1682, Lord Grey noted that 'no men of quality or interest, who had a common understanding, would undertake such an affair, without a provision of arms, and other necessaries for war.'[12] It was when these arrangements to secure the country where linked to the Rye House Plot of 1683, that the Whig leadership was forced escape into exile in Holland, or die as martyrs.[13] Once in Amsterdam, the English Whigs joined with the Scots covenanters and commenced preparing for an invasion of Britain which was set for Michaelmas 1684.[14]

Those in this new Anglo-Scottish Whig cabal understood that it was only by creating new model armies that could they match the small British Army on the battlefield. As the leadership intended to launch a three-pronged assault on Britain; one in Scotland, another in Cheshire, and the last in the west of England, they needed Generals. Men that could command loyalty, and who could mould men and equipment into a creditable armies. Of the two factions, Scottish Whigs had a clear head start, many of them had been in exile since 1679. They also had a willing and experience nobleman to lead them, the Earl of Argyll. By using his connections, the Earl had raised 10,000 livres,[15] ready to buy arms and equipment.

However, it was a different story in the English camp. By early 1684, the English did not have a general to rally or organise an army. They had asked the old Cromwellian, General Ludlow, to lead them but he had rejected the call of the good old cause. The regicide preferred staying safely in Switzerland to leading a new republican army. So, the English Whigs found themselves leaderless.[16] To make matters worse, Government agents had uncovered the 1684 plot, and Whitehall acted by seizing weapons and making countless arrests. This forced the Whigs to postpone the invasions to the spring of 1685. As fate would have it, the death of Charles II accelerated the Whig's preparations, and gave the English Whigs a willing and very credible commander, the Duke of Monmouth.[17]

In very early March 1685[18], the Whigs high command met for the first time at Mr Dare's house in Amsterdam.[19] Everyone that sat around the table understood that, even with massive popular support, no army could fight without arms, and nor could it be an effective weapon without structure. They all

---

12 BL, Add MS 30277, f.18.
13 The leader of the Whig movement, Lord William Russell was an actively involved in these plans, but was linked by a paid witness to the plot to kill the King and along with other Whigs was executed in 1683.
14 September, see Wade's narrative.
15 BL, Add MS 30277, f.36 Grey states that 7,000 of this had come from Mrs Smith, a rich widow and close friend of Argyll.
16 BL, Harley 6845, f.269.
17 Another popular myth is that somehow Monmouth was an unwilling leader. It is true that Monmouth was first approached by the Scottish Whigs in February but at this point he had already started talking to the English Whigs. At the beginning of March, Monmouth convinced the Scots that he was a creditable leader and just a few days later the Duke met Argyll. After this Monmouth was the driving force behind the creation of the English Army.
18 Possibly 3 March 1685.
19 *Negotiations de Monsieur le Comte d'Avaux en Hollande*, Vol. IV, (Paris, 1753), p.297.

knew they would be faced by the two solid, but small standing armies inherited by the usurper King James II/ VII. Although, these had been paid for with Louis XIV's French golden livre, most of the high-ranking government officers had all fought under Monmouth and received promotion through his actions. Monmouth knew his enemy, and therefore want would be needed to defeat them, namely arms, ammunition, officers, and money.

There is another romantic perception fostered by the 'pitchfork army' that needs to be dispelled, and this is that the Whigs had no experienced officers. As individuals both Monmouth, and Argyll, had vast amount of personal military expertise to draw upon. Monmouth had been captain general of the British Army that fought and defeated the Scot's Covenanters at Bothwell Bridge in 1679. Before this, as general of the day, Monmouth had led the assault on Maastricht, which as a result capitulated in July 1673. After this feat of arms, had command of the British Army in French service, until the nation switch allegiances to the United Provence's in 1677. Ultimately, this resulted in Monmouth commanding the English Brigade to victory under his cousin, William, Prince of Orange at the Battle of St Denis.

Monmouth was not alone, as arrayed around the table at Mr Dare's house and waiting outside sat vast number of veteran officers. First of these was the Earl of Argyll. By 1679 Argyll was a leading opponent of the Duke of York but had avoided being pulled into the defeat of the Scots Covenanters[20] at Bothwell Bridge. Before this Argyll that had fought for King Charles II at the Battle of Worcester in 1651 and after this, he was one of the leaders involved in the Glencairne revolt against Cromwell in Scotland during the 1650's. During this campaign, Argyll faced two old Cromwellian officers who sat at the same table in Amsterdam. These were Richard Rumbold and Abraham Holmes. As an officer Rumbold had guarded the scaffold upon which Charles I meet his end and then fought for parliament at the Battle of Worcester. Alongside the old Cromwellian, were other experience officers including Captain Samuel Venner, Captain Robert Fletcher, Captain Robert Bruce, and Captain Edward Matthews, all of whom held commissions in the army of Brandenburg. Then there were the disaffected Whig officers in the English Brigade in Dutch service. It was in these regiments that Captain Parson, Captain Foulkes, Ensign Fox, and Ensign Baddington all held commissions. Finally, hiding back in England were old soldiers like Colonel Danvers, Colonel Bovett and Captain Robert Parrot. The Whigs were also joined by Colonel Brandt, the Count of Horne,[21] a Dutch officer on leave from the Prince of Orange's Army and the artillery officer Captain Anton Buyse from Brandenburg. To this extensive pool of men, can be added the 300 hundred Scots soldiers waiting in the streets of Utrecht, Amsterdam, and Rotterdam for the call to arms.[22] None of these men could be called inexperienced 'amateurs', as portrayed by so many historians.

Many of the Scots commanders knew, through personal experience, the lessons from failed rebellions, while other had been with Monmouth when he defeated those same Scotsmen at Bothwell Bridge. The lesson that had been learnt, and this was that it they would need structured, disciplined, and well-equipped armies. The council agreed that they would lead liberating armies in the upcoming campaigns, and to do this the Whigs needed to buy, store and transport military equipment. The armies would require modelling with a command structure able to arm and train the anticipated recruits.

---

20   Ultimately, the Scots Covenanters combine politically with the English Whigs during the 1680's and merge in a common aim after 1683.
21   Koninklijke Bibliotheek, Amsterdam, KW Pflt 12343.
22   *Negotiations de Monsieur le Comte d'Avaux en Hollande*, Vol. IV, (Paris, 1753), p.291.

By mid-March 1685, Monmouth and Argyll had agreed on the invasion plan, and Whig agents had set out to find all the officers and equipment needed for the new model armies. With his planning well underway, and his 10,000 livres, Argyll had procured arms, ammunition, and powder. In a visit to Argyll in April 1685, Wade estimated that the Scots had 'about 8000 arms, & 500 Barrels of Gunpowder, wch cost about 9000*l*'.[23] All this was securely stored in Amsterdam warehouses, and ready to transport to Scotland in the three ships that had been hired. One of these was the 26-gun *Anna*, a sixth-rate frigate, which was ready to protect the fleet and would carry most of the veteran soldiers. The *Anna* was joined by two merchant vessels the *David* and the *Sophie*. These would contain most of the weapons, and the smaller *Sophie* had the dangerous task of carrying the barrels of black powder. However, the English Whigs had not yet started to the procurement process and needed to move quickly to be ready for the invasion date which had been set as 23 April 1685.

To get the job done quickly, Monmouth split his agents into three areas of focus: logistics, procurement, and recruitment. Captain Foulkes was sent into the British garrisons to enrol more dissatisfied NCO's and junior officers. Lord Grey was sent to Amsterdam to hire ships for the invasion and co-ordinated activities with the with the Scots. While the Duke used his Dutch mercantile connections to secure the warehousing and transports needed to store the military equipment. Beyond this, other men like Benjamin Hewling and Nathaniel Wade were set out to purchase the arms and equipment needed for the army. In the seventeenth century, as today, the supply of military arms and equipment in times of peace was procurement exercise, with agents going to the manufacturers, or finding stockpiles of older weapons in dusty storerooms and offering the best price.

The assumption made by many historians, is that Monmouth arrived with just a small quantity of arms, with the rest of the weaponry coming from the local population in the shape of 'pitchforks.' Therefore, the resulting use of scythes, sticks, rusty swords, antique muskets, and other base arms, does not need much by the way of warehousing or logistics. This general view appears to be supported by the assurances sent by Major Wildman, leader of the English Whigs in London to Monmouth. In his one of his letters, Wildman writes 'that there was no need for arms, the people were well armed.'[24] However, Wildman was not referring to farm yard tools, but the stores of weapons being held in secret locations across England, first gathered up in 1681, and extended over the next few years. In early 1684, when the Government uncovered the planned September uprisings, and the Earl of Sunderland had ordered the seizure of weapons from all 'persons disaffected to the Governmt.'[25] The resulting hoard makes an impressive list, with over 1,000 muskets, pikes, pistols, swords and carbines.[26] Yet this was just the tip of the iceberg as more weapons had been hidden across the country. This is highlighted when Monmouth reached Chard, and a party of horse under Quartermaster Thompson visited the home of Mr Prideaux. After having dinner with the gentleman, the officer collected 'muskets, carbines and a blunerbuss, amounting to about fifteen or sixteen [pieces] … about ten or twelve half-pikes,' all of which had been in storage waiting for the invasion.[27]

Nevertheless, Monmouth and his officers were experienced enough to know that they needed regimented equipment, especially muskets for the infantry. Therefore, nothing was going to be left to chance. Each firearm needed the correct bullet mould, and these were found in each case of muskets from the manufacturer. As without this simple tool, even the best and latest firelock musket was just an

---

23 BL, Harley 6845, f.270r.
24 BL, Harley 6845, f.271r
25 NA, WO 55/1760, f.1.
26 See Table 1.
27 BL, Add MS 62453, f.50, f.56 & f.58.

expensive wooden club. As each pair of musketeer files needed to share the bullet mould, ensuring they had the same bore of musket was critical. The greater the variety of muskets, the harder it was logistically to ensure every soldier could fight effectively on the battlefield. As a result, Monmouth ignored Wildman's assurances of ample weaponry being available and therefore he sent his agents out to buy what was needed for the army. This covered everything from muskets and pikes, to drums, colours, powder, shot, flints, even uniforms.

The Scottish Whigs had been luckily enough to buy everything straight from merchants, and deliveries had gone to their warehouses in Amsterdam. From these quayside buildings they could be easily loaded into the ships for transportation, but once the right paperwork was in place. With the Scots settling on documents showing destination for the arms was in the Nordics.[28] However, for Monmouth's agents the procurement process became harder after the death of Charles II, as not only had the Scots acquired most of the ready weapons and powder, the English Whigs were faced with red tape from the Dutch state. They also fell under the watchful eyes of French and British spies, and it is these untapped reports that shine a spotlight on the Whig's procurement activities.

It is highly probable that Monmouth used his family connections, along with his ability to speak Dutch and French,[29] to raise the credit needed to secure the much-needed warehousing in Utrecht and Rotterdam.[30] Monmouth also used a web of sympathetic Dutchmen to transport any newly procured equipment to these storage locations. It is important to understand that without this vital storage and transport network in place, any weapons purchased would never make it to England. With the Scots having stripped local suppliers, the Whigs looked beyond the United Provinces, towards France,[31] but especially to Flanders for the stocks of arms and ammunition needed. After his exile in 1683, Monmouth had taken up service in the Imperial Spanish Army and spent time in Flanders. Over the next few weeks Whig agents bought up surplus arms in Antwerp, Brussels, and Liege. Some of this secret traffic came to the attention of Captain Tilliers, who wrote to Skelton on May 23 that he'd seen 'several [cases] laden with arms, as muskets, carbines, and pistols … eighty cases laden with all sorts, as musketts, carbines, pistols, pikes, speares, halbards, partisans &ea:'[32] being shipped to Rotterdam on a barge. These caseloads of muskets, bundles of pikes, bags of defensive armour, and baskets of swords, travelled via water to Dordrecht, before being transferred into wagons to finish the journey to Rotterdam or Utrecht.

Beyond this, Hewling was busy buying another important item of equipment and it is this aspect of the military planning that turned the rabble into an army – uniforms. The evidence for this comes from a number of references, the first is when Monmouth's men disembarked at Lyme when an eyewitness reported that 'as all or most of the Rebells had at their Landing the late Duke was in Purple.'[33] This is supported by a report from the French ambassador at the Hague, who wrote about the Whigs having 'made a lot of purple-red coats [qu'ils avoient fait faire quantité de casaques d'un rouge couleur

---

28 BL, Add MS 41817, f.35.
29 Monmouth was born in Rotterdam and spend the first seven years in and around the Dutch court at the Hague. Furthermore, it is often overlooked by historians that his aunt was married into a Dutch mercantile family from Rotterdam, giving the Duke access to connections, shipping, and warehousing not available to other Englishmen.
30 BL, Egerton MS 1527, shows the shipping symbols for 10 merchants plus names and addresses of some of his English & Dutch connections.
31 It is possible, but unsupported, that Monmouth's four 3-pound cannon came from France.
32 BL, Add MS 41817 f.51.
33 BL, Harley 6845, f.254r.

de pourpre]'.[34] However, there is a very telling English spy report dated May 17 that pulls together the logistic behind the creation of the uniform coats but also the network put in place by the Whigs. In his report an agent writes that 'Mr Hewling, the son of Benjamin Hewling mercht. in Colman Street went from Utrecht on Thursday morning for Amsterdam. It is he who tooke care of the making the purple coats, lined with red, for the souldiers that shall be imployed in the Rebells service.'[35] What is clear from this information, is that both the Scottish and English fleets carried uniforms, and that the officers and some of the men wore these coats during the campaign.

The other activity underway by Whig agents was the recruitment of experienced junior officers, from the regiments in foreign service. For the Scottish expedition, Argyll had his pool of 300 veterans, many with commissions in Dutch or Brandenburger regiments. However, Monmouth knew he needed more officers and sent Captain Foulkes, and Ensign Fox into the garrison taverns of s-Hertogenbosch. It was in these drinking holes that Foulkes found a willing group of newly unemployed British officers from the English Brigade. As fortune would have it, these men had been kicked out of service after King James presented Orange with a list of English officers and dangerous citizens in February 1685. Furthermore, King James demanded that they should be expelled from the United Provinces. Luckily for Monmouth, this action created a small group of disaffected officers and gentlemen. However, Foulkes looked beyond these men and went around the tables to recruit NCOs with the promise of a promotion, and good pay. The cover was that they would be joining a new 'Brandenburger' company. Such were Foulkes' exploits, that he gained some notoriety in Whitehall and Paris, as Major Gillycuddys report explains 'Capta Foulkes came to the town, where he stayed some time, and has perswaded some young Gen:tlemen of Sr Henry Bellassis Regimt; to goo along with him; telling them he was made Major to the Duke of Brandenburge Guardes, and he was to raise a strong Compay.'[36]

While Captain Foulkes was busy in s-Hertogenbosch, three small merchantmen had been hired secretly by Lord Grey. However, this was not the only method the Whigs would use to send weapons into England. During April, caseloads of pistols, carbines and muskets arrived in London in the holds of merchant vessels sailing from Rotterdam.[37] Once unload at the London docks they were stacked in carts and delivered to eager groups of sympathisers in the west and around Chester.[38] By the time this activity came to the attention of government spies, Argyll had departed and Whitehall assumed that the shipments were heading to Scotland,[39] and ordered all carts heading north to be searched. They found nothing. Another indicator of transportation of equipment before the landing at Lyme was the arrest, near Taunton on June 5, of the merchant Mr Hewling (Senior). It must be speculated that 'he who tooke care of the making the purple coats' delivered both equipment and/ or messages into the town, a week before Monmouth's landing.

With a smaller invasion, relying in part on equipment being shipped separately, Monmouth had only hired the *Straw* and two other small merchant ships.[40] However, just hours after Argyll's departure,

34 *Negotiations de Monsieur le Comte d'Avaux en Hollande*, Vol. IV, (Paris: 1753), p.363. The historian Roberts translated this as red coats faced with purple.
35 BL, Add MS 41812, f.72.
36 BL, Add MS 41817, f.51.
37 BL, Add MS 41817, f.38.
38 The same method of distribution was used by Monmouth's father to supply weapons to the Royalist prior to the Penrudduck Uprising in 1655. This was the rebellion within which that many of the older Whigs, such as Major Holmes, Captain Parrot and on the opposing side, Colonel Bovett had played an active part.
39 NA, SP 44/336, f.103.
40 BL, Add MS 41812, f.66 'what can be done agst 4 ships?'.

HMS Sandedous arrived in Amsterdam and it became clear to Monmouth that a warship was needed to protect the fleet. To do this, the Duke pawned his remaining assets and his agent, Mr Daniel Le Blon came into play. Within days, the Whigs hired a private fifth-rate frigate called the *Heldenerberg* commanded by the pro-Whig Captain Cornelius van Brakell.[41] The vessel was sea-worthy, but in need of a refit and new armament. Amazingly the Whigs were able to buy and supply captain Brakell with '26: Guns; wth 10:- 6 poundrs 10:- 3 pundrs & 6:- 1 poundrs guns'[42] and hire crew. This is another demonstration of the logistical prowess of the Whigs, and the silent support offered by the Dutch state for the enterprise.[43] While outwardly enforcing James demands to stop the Whigs activities, Orange and his magistrates allowed Monmouth to buy arms and hire Dutch seafarers. Making ready the *Helderenberg* delayed the invasion fleet sailing by three weeks, giving Captain Foulkes more valuable recruiting time in 'den Bosch.

Loading equipment onto a '*lighter*' for transportation c.1684. Authors collection

By the last week of May the English invasion was ready, yet one problem remained. As a result of Argyll's fleet leaving unhindered on May 2, new legislation was in place stopping arms and ammunition being shipped from the United Provinces. Once more Le Blon came to the rescue by finding a loophole in the legislation. It was discovered that the embargo did not restrict the transfer of equipped within Holland or to ships not in the harbour. So, the Whig fleet put out to sea and anchored off the Texel. Then small inshore vessels were loaded with the stores, weapons, and men, and taken to the

---

41   BL, Add MS 41822, f.255.
42   BL, Add MS 41822, f.262.
43   Sir John Dalrymple, *Memoirs of Great Britain and Ireland*, Vol. III, 4th Edition, (Dublin: David Hay, 1773), p.20, 25 August 1685, James complained to Orange 'As for the names of any of the magistrates of Amsterdam, when I can get any authentic proofs against them, I shall let you have it, which, I fear, will be hard to be got, though 'tis certain some of them knew of the Duke of Monmouth's design'.

waiting ships. However, the winds turned against the Whigs, and this extra effort took up even more precious time, adding another week to the departure date.

The first ship ready was the *Straw*, and with her destination being Bridgwater, Bristol, or Chester, around May 22 she sailed west.[44] Unfortunately, on May 31 *HMS Tiger* was cruising off the Isle of Wight when the captain spotted a 'dutch flyboat.'[45] After a short chase, the *Tiger* intercepted the *Straw*, and her important cargo. In one reports the small transport was described as:

> a ship going to joyne with Argyle, with 5000 stand of mo armes in it, (but Argyle had already mo armes then he had men to give them to, unlesse they be designed for some insurrection in Wales, or some other place in the West of England, wher they are much addicted to Monmouth, and disaffected to this King,) and some Dutch officers.[46]

Back in Amsterdam, English agents and the Ambassador had ordered the Dutch officials to seize the *Helderenberg*. However, the paper was arrived in time for the spies to watch the English Whig fleet cross the Texel into the North Sea. They sailed on May 28, with 80 officers and mercenaries together with the pilot John Wootler but without Monmouth. The Duke was still at the Hague until May 24, and then after a round-about route which took the government agents off guard, Monmouth reached the invasion fleet by rowing boat on May 29. The following day with 'ye Helderen Bergh put out (as a Man-of-War) Jack, Pendant & flagg' the English invasion began.

It is hard to estimate the total number of weapons purchased and transported to England. As a guide, spies copied the shipping manifests for the *Anna*, *Sophie*, and *David*, from these it is clear the Scots had over 10,000 muskets plus 16 canons.[47] This is collaborated, with the reports of the stores found in Eilean Dearg Castle after its capture. There are several contemporary references that indicate that the arms and ammunition carried to Lyme, was about half the number transported by Argyll. Oldmixon wrote that Monmouth landed with 'arms for about 5,000 men, horse and foot'[48] and this would appear to be correct. Under interrogation, the paymaster, Captain Goodenough estimated that Monmouth 'brought nely 2500 arms.'[49] In his narrative, Nathanial Wade indicates that Monmouth had 'orders with my self to provide two Small ships, and about 1,500 foot arms, 1,500 cuirasses, 4 Pieces of Artillery mounted on field carriages, 200 as I take it barrels of gunpowder, with some small quantity of Granado shells match and other things.'[50] Lord Grey provides another manifest with '1460

---

44 It is not clear if the *Straw* was sailing to England or Scotland, but her presence indicates more than the landing at Lyme were planned.
45 NA, ADM 51/4369, ff.20–21.
46 *Historical Selections from the Manuscripts of Sir John Lauder of Fountainhall*, Volume First, (Edinburgh: Bannatyne Club, 1837), p.169.
47 See Table 3 for an example manifest.
48 John Oldmixon, *The History of England*, (London: Pemberton, 1730), p.701, too many dismiss Oldmixon figures as his text does not reflect the historical myth. However, as a boy Oldmixon lived in Bridgwater, and witnessed Monmouth's Army march out of the town on July 5, and the fugitives return in the early hours of July 6 after the fight at Sedgemoor. Therefore, his account must be taken at face value.
49 BL, Lansdown 1152, f.243.
50 BL, Harl. 6845, f.271r, Monmouth put Wade in charge of the loading of arms and equipment into one of the transports in Amsterdam, and then its unloading at Lyme. See Table 4.

suites of defensive Armes, 100 musquetts, and bandaliers: 500 Pikes: as many swords, 250 barrells of powder besides what was provided for ye frigate, a small number of double Carbines and pistols.'[51]

Plainly these accounts differ, but they would, as each writer only saw the stores for which they were responsible. While Wade talks of two ships, Grey describes the Frigate, therefore neither saw the whole inventory.[52] However, there are other overlooked accounts that detail the number of weapons. In the confession of Richard Goodenough, the army's paymaster states that they had 2,500 infantry arms.[53] Another eyewitness report comes from a spy who visited Lyme on June 12. The man talked to an officer who had landed with Monmouth and this nameless character stated that 'be they Twenty or Thirty Thousand he [Monmouth] has Armes enough for them all.'[54] This was clearly bravado, but it does show the confidence that army had enough equipment for the expected recruits.

A waggon on the road carrying goods or arms c.1685. Authors collection

Monmouth's servant Williams, who told his captors 'that 1500 horse arms & about 2000 other arms were also ship'd there.'[55] This could be in the ships or by transport and if we return to the home of Mr Prideaux on June 14, Quartermaster Thompson let it slip over supper that 'they designed for Taunton where their arms would be much increased.' Indicating that Monmouth knew of arms being stored in Taunton. To this growing list of weapons can be added equipment from the Militia,[56] the arms

---

51 BL, Add. MS 30077, f.28r. Please note that 100 is the correct amount in both the original manuscript and the 1754 printed version. This is in the middle of the line and is not an error as indicated by other historians. Grey had been assigned with organising and hiring the transports for England, and as the officer to command the horse, would have been responsible for loading the equipment needed for the Whig cavalry. See Table 5.
52 Especially as neither list would not have filled one ship, let alone the three that sailed together to Lyme Regis.
53 BL, Lansdown 1152, f.243.
54 BL, Harley 6845, f.254r.
55 BL, Lansdowne 1152, f.237.
56 BL, Harley 6845, f.287.

collected in Somerset during 1684 that were still in the Taunton armoury on May 9[57] and retrieved after the Castle was stormed on June 17.[58] Finally, there was a late bonus when Monmouth arrived at Wells on July 1, to find wagons full of new weapons left by Kirke's Regiment.[59] One final pointer to Monmouth's having arms enough for over 5,000 men comes when the army marched out of Lyme with between 1,500 and 2,000 soldiers,[60] due to a shortage of wagons they left behind '40 barrels of powder, and back, brest, and head pieces for near 5000 men.'[61] As this volume of defensive armours do not appear on any manifests of shipment list, clearly Wade and Grey haven't seen everything.

One final pointer to the number of weapons brought over by Monmouth is the *Straw*. If this flyboat held 5,000 arms, and Argyll's three ships carried more than 10,000 weapons, evidently there was more equipment than Wade or Grey acknowledged. In Monmouth's fleet of a Carrick, a Dogger[62] and the *Helderenberg*, the tally must come close to Goodenough's estimate of weapons for 2,500 foot, and possibly 1,500 for the horse. Conceivably, as many as 2,000 firearms could have been shipped to Taunton before the landings, and with this we go beyond the 5,000 estimated by Oldmixon. To this we can add five to 600 scythes, plus around a thousand weapons captured from the militia and taken from the armouries.

To support this estimated and give fresh insight into the true nature of Monmouth's Army, once more agents provide the missing information. On the wet Thursday afternoon of 25 June, rather than being at Frome with the pitchfork armed mob, Monmouth was at Keynsham, some 20 miles away. The Duke had just marched across the River Avon at Keynsham bridge and had drawn up the Army up in Battalia on the Gloucestershire side of the river, on Sydenham Mead. This large array of soldiers made a fine spectacle for the bystanders and the following morning one of these, Mr Cheswick, wrote to the Earl of Feversham.[63] In this letter to James' General, Cheswick gave a full description of Monmouth's Army. He noted that the Whigs were 'above 1,000 horse and about 8,000 foot, 8 field pieces … his men some well-armed, others indifferent, and some not at all, only having an old sword or a sticke in their hand ; however, I observed many musketts and other ammunition in their carriages.' This contemporary account provides a more realistic view of the Whigs, one that is more akin to Clarendon's picture of King Charles I's Army at Edgehill, than of those men collecting at Frome with 'pitchforks'. This is a vastly different picture from the one published days later in the London Gazette and the one repeated ever since from Frome.

Mr Cheswick's statement demonstrates that the Whigs had outgrown their quartermaster's ability to supply weapons to all the new recruits. While historical blindness has only focused on the unarmed followers, it has ignored the 6,000 men equipped for war. Critically, this total number is close to the estimated number of foot arms shipped or acquired in England. Therefore, this description of Monmouth's Army at Keynsham is invaluable. There are some errors, eight guns rather than the actual four, but just 14 days after their landing at Lyme the Duke's Army was larger than King Charles

---

57 Northumberland Papers, MS 288, f.7. See Table 2.
58 BL, Harley 6845, f.287.
59 *The Manuscripts of the Earl of Dartmouth*, Eleventh Report, (London: Historical Manuscripts Commission, 1887) p.128, 'that the arms last received from Whitehall were all lost at Wells' Kirke to Dartmouth, July 13 1685. This many have been as many as 250 muskets and 100 pikes.
60 *Earl of Dartmouth*, Eleventh Report, p.16.
61 Narcissus Luttrell, *A Brief Historical Relation of State Affairs*, Vol. I (Oxford: Oxford University Press, 1857), p.349.
62 NA, ADM 106/374, f.265.
63 The General in command of all King James II's forces in England.

I's forces a fortnight into their 1642 campaign. What this intelligence demonstrates is that midway through the western venture, at the core of the army there were around 3,500 well equipped soldiers. With another 2,500 or so, only had their main arm, of pike, scythe, or musket. Possibly 600 of these were the infamous 'scythe-men' raised at Taunton. Finally, there were around 1,000 to 2,000 individuals simply following Monmouth in the baggage train. However, it is clear there is no shortage of firearms as 'many musketts' are still in carts, although this could indicate a lack of bandoleers or the other accessories needed to discharge a seventeenth century firearm. Alternatively, the weapons still needed to be issued. This does not portray is our classic picture of the 'pitchfork army' but is very similar to Clarendon's account of the Royalist army at Edgehill in 1642.

In the archives there is another and more detailed description of Whig troopers. This is found in letters written by government soldiers after the clash at Ashill on June 19. As this was the first encounter between the regular government army and Monmouth's, it had some importance for both sides. It came after Lord Churchill had advanced to Chard with two troops from the Royal Regiment of Horse, or Oxford's Blues. After arriving in the town, Churchill sent out patrols to locate the Whig Army, and one of these was a division from Captain Littleton's troop, under Lieutenant Monoux. It was their baptism of fire, and the troopers were well trained, armed, and enthusiastic to fight. Each man carried a long sword, a pair of pistols, a carbine, and wore defensive armour of back, breast and a pot helmet. As Monoux covered the ground near Ashill, in the distance they saw about 14 troopers from Monmouth's Horse. Without hesitation Monoux seized the opportunity to demonstrate his men's superiority. Expecting the enemy to flee, the Oxford Blues closed as if to give chase. However, Cornet Legg commanding the Whigs, was also keen to test his men and pull off a quick victory. Therefore, both sides tossed caution to the wind and cantered into battle, both sides were eager to demonstrate their abilities in this opening encounter. As with most cavalry combats, it was a short and bloody affair, with the officers from both sides killed by pistol shots in the first contact. Then as Whig reinforcements arrived, the government troopers retreated to Chard. However, they took back some valuable information. Once in the safety of the town, they reported to their commander that the enemy 'were all in Armour & their Carbines & Pistols were all wth double Barrills.' This does not sound like soldiers from a 'pitchfork army', especially as they were better armed and equipped than the Royal Regiment of Horse.

If taken in isolation, the Ashill report is easy to dismiss, but this episode the supported by logistical audit trail. It is this that shows the Whig's procurement process in action. Agents reports follow the purchase of the weapons described at Ashill as 'Carbines & Pistols were all wth double Barrills.'[64] The next reference to these weapons is in Lord Grey list as 'small number of double Carbines and pistols'[65] Before this, on May 22 a spy writes that 'the Pistols with four barrels are of a very rare invention is 70 pounds a pair…the carbines with two barrels'.[66] A day earlier, another spy wrote from Utrecht that 'the pair of four-barrel pistols are ready.'[67] Clearly, the English government were looking for more information on those weapons, as 10 days before, again from Utrecht, Skelton is told that 'the weapons made in this town are muskets, rifles, pistols, and pistols, the pistols have four small cannons[68] to fit in your

---

64 BL, Add MS 38012, f.3.
65 BL, Add MS 30277, f.28r.
66 BL, Add MS 41817, f.47, 'Pistolts a quatre Canons sont d'une invention fort rare est de 70 Livres le pair … les Carabines a deux canons'.
67 BL, Add MS 41817, f.65, 'pour quand le pair des pistolets a quatre Canons seront prets'.
68 Modern translation is 'barrels', this is from the French *canon* or barrel.

pocket.'⁶⁹ Yet the first reference is found on May 7, when another agent writes that these weapons where 'made in this City of the Invention of the late Prince Ruperts.'⁷⁰ Therefore, the weapons seen at Ashill are no random purchase by a few individuals, but can be traced back through shipment, storage and possibly to their manufacture in Heidelberg on the Rhine. This journey is good illustration of the Whigs and seventeenth century logistics in action.

Once the logistics to supply weapons is in place, seventeenth century modelling turns a mob of poorly lead peasants, or bunch of disorganised lowlanders, into raw but disciplined armies. The term model has become generalised and linked to the New Model Army of Fairfax and later Cromwell. However, the process of modelling or remodelling is the act of creating a military structure. To understand modelling of an army, one of the foundations is the establishment of an infantry companies or cavalry troops. From these elements, battalions, squadrons, and regiments are built. However, these formations are not random acts but planned before weapons are purchased or officers rerolled. Using Wade's narrative as a guide, each Whig company of foot was to have a captain, two lieutenants and an ensign.⁷¹ This is the most telling aspects of the military preparations as weapons and uniforms can be bought on speculation, but colours need modelling. While an officer corps can be expanded during a campaign, to make regimental colours requires a deep understanding of the structure and model of the Army.

Colours, standards, or cornets are an important part of the seventeenth century army, they are more than 'a rag on a pole', they are a core part of the modelling of a unit. In addition they not easily created; Colours need handy needlework, dyes, designs, and above all time. To reinforce the popular myth of Monmouth's 'pitchfork army', the traditionally view is that the 'maids' of Taunton made all the colours and presented these to the army on June 19. A tall order, even if we remove Monmouth's dark green standard raised at Lyme. For 13 maids to make 26 colours in just seven days is an amazing feat, especially without knowing the model of the army. Unfortunately, once more historical blindness has ignored the spy reports coming from Holland before the invasion sailed. These reports document a good number of colours with mottos for the Scots such as 'For God and Religion against Popery, Tyranny, Arbitrary Government, and Erastianism',⁷² 'For the Protestant Religion', 'Against Popery, Prelacy, and Erastianism',⁷³ 'For God and Religion',⁷⁴ 'Against Popery, Prelary & Erastianism',⁷⁵ 'Against Papismum, Episiopatum & Erashianismum'⁷⁶, 'God forward us', 'From Popery, Heresy, and Seizure, Good Lord deliver us',⁷⁷ and they also detail English colours with 'For Religion & Liberty',⁷⁸ 'For God & our Privileges'⁷⁹ and 'For God freedom and Religion'.⁸⁰

---

69 BL, Add MS 41812, f.77, 'Les armes faites dans cette ville sont des mousquets, carabins, pistoles, et Pistolets, les Pistoles ont quatre Canons asses petits pour les melser dans la poche'.
70 BL, Add MS 41812, f.66, 'sont fais dans cette Ville de l'Invention du feu Prince Ruperts'.
71 BL, Harley 6845, f.274.
72 *Historical Selections from the Manuscripts of Sir John Lauder of Fountainhall*, Volume First, (Edinburgh: Bannatyne Club, 1837), p.177.
73 John Erskine, *The Journal of the Hon. John Erskine of Carnock*, (Edinburgh:1893), p.119.
74 BL, Add MS 41822, f.242.
75 BL, Add MS 38012, f.3.
76 BL, Add MS 41817, f.5.
77 National Archive SP Ireland 351, f.26.
78 *Negotiations de Monsieur le Comte d'Avaux en Hollande*, Vol. V, (Paris: 1753), p.21.
79 BL, Add MS 41817, f.151.
80 BL, Add MS 41812, f.65.

Importantly, some the English colours are described as 'blew.' It is therefore very evident that as Bovett's Taunton Blue Regiment was formed at Taunton on June 19, the maids did not make the colours. The more likely situation was that maids were given the colours to present, and only made one which was 'Golden Flag JR, a crown & fringes lace round.'[81] Once it is understood the colours were made before the landings, and Monmouth's own standards are removed, 25 colours remain. With this information the model of Whig army is discovered, five regiments, each with five companies. This is no random act as it matches Argyll's modelling at Tarbert on May 28, where three regiments of foot, each with five companies were raised.[82]

With the removal of the final foundation of the 'pitchfork army' myth, the parallel with his grandfather forming his army at Nottingham in 1642 comes into focus. As the *Helderenberg* neared Lyme,[83] Monmouth commissioned his officers. They would form the four regiments of foot at Lyme.[84] The morning after the landing, Monmouth's dark a green standard with his motto 'Fear Nothing but God'[85] was erected in the field on the edge of Lyme. As the eager men arrived, they were greeted by smart officers dressed in purple coats with red linings, while below the standard was a table and a clerk.[86] The new recruits must have formed a queue, then wrote down their name, or made there mark, before the clerk gave then a note. This detailed the formation they were to join, after which the new soldier was taken to a group of recruits waiting for a messenger. Once a dozen or more men were gathered, the messenger took them to the town hall,[87] where they were issued a pike or musket and bandoleer. With his name noted, the new soldier was sent off to one of the new companies of a hundred men[88] being formed on the edge of town. Once they reached their new officers, any ex-soldiers or militia men would become an NCO and they could start weapons training. If a man arrived mounted he was sent into town for pistols, carbine, and armour before joining his troop of Horse. The best mounted troopers were issued with two quad-barrelled pistols, a double-barrelled carbine and a back and breast plate before joining Major Manley's troop.

The creation of the Whig Army was a well thought out enlistment process not dissimilar to the formation of any other seventeenth century battalion or army. This modelling followed the structure agreed in Amsterdam and once enough companies were at full strength, the Regiments started to be formed. The first was Monmouth's own Regiment of Foot, commanded by Colonel Samuel Venner, with Major Wade and approximately 500 soldiers. Then came Colonel Holmes' Green Regiment, with the same number and Colonel Foulkes' White Regiment with about 350 soldiers. The last raised at Lyme was Colonel Matthews' Yellow Regiment and was initially command by Major Fox, as Matthews'

---

81 BL, Harley 7006, f.195r.
82 *A Selection of Papers of the Earls of Marchmont*, Volume. III (London: Murray, 1831), p.43. Although, it is clear he had planned for at least eight battalions, as commissions were held back until the estimate 8,000 recruits appeared.
83 BL, Harley 6845, f.274. 'Whilst wee were on shipboard wee received serverall commissions from ye Duke in paper'.
84 The fifth, or Blue Regiment was to be raised in Taunton.
85 BL, Add MS 31956, f.2. 'They continued in Lyme listing associats (which every moment came to them) under their now display'd Colours which are a deep Green, inscribed wth letters of Gold [Fear nothing but God]'
86 BL, Harley 6845, f.254r, 'the Standard set-up and the late Duke standing by and a writer with him listing men'.
87 BL, Harley 6845, f.274r.
88 BL, Harley 6845, f.285.

was still making his way from London.[89] The formation of the Blue Regiment would be delayed until they reached Taunton, where Colonel Bovett and some of the officers waited.

In Scotland, Argyll followed a similar process, with three regiments of five companies, each of 100 soldiers, being created. These were Colonel Sir Duncan Campbell of Archinbreck's, Colonel Robert Elphinson of Lapness's, and then the Englishman Colonel John Ayloff's. Unlike Monmouth's Army there is also the mention of a Regiment of Horse with three troops under Colonel Richard Rumbold, although the troop that came from Campbeltown was described by Erskine as 'tho the Horse were but good for Dragoons'.[90] The newly enlisted soldiers also received firelock muskets, and the companies from Holland had both special muskets and halberds.[91] This was no random act, the colours, weapons, uniforms and modelling were agreed in March 1685, months before the invasions took place.

By the time Monmouth reached Taunton, there is no question that the Whigs had outgrown the regimented equipment stored in Holland. However, this does not mean that the core of his army was not well armed, nor does this indicate the army was a mob of 'untrained amateurs'. Monmouth landed at Lyme with the weapons and colours need to form five regiments of foot, each with five companies of 100 men. Together with enough swords, pistols, carbines, and defensive arms for 10 squadrons of three troops of horse, each of 50 soldiers. These men were well armed, drilled and had commissioned officers. There is one final act that breaks 'pitchfork army' myth. Monmouth's Army was enlisted and possibly even paid after the first week. This is supported by the statement of the captured Whig Captain Robert Bruce at his trial in Scotland in February 1686. In this he declares that the 'Duke did sometym pay the souldiers who wer in rebellione with him.'[92] While Roger Morrice, in his now deciphered diaries, writes that 'the Rebels pay for all they take.'[93] This is no longer a mob or rabble but a professional army.

With the prejudice or blindness created by the 'pitchfork army' myth removed, the Whigs demonstrated the art of modelling of an army, and uniquely, this is from scratch. The first step was to define the basic army element of the company or troop, and after this the battalion structure. Then the warehousing space needed to be hired, before the weapons, ammunition, colours, and uniforms could be purchased and stored. To ready the population, and enable the uprisings, shipments of arms were sent to a network of supporters. After this, transports were hired to ferry the equipment to the landing beaches and Frigates needed to protect the fleet. While the procurement process was in full swing, recruiting officers scoured the Inns and Taverns of the garrison towns for disaffected soldiers to strengthen the experience of the corps. Agents then travelled into hostile land with a date and place to muster. Just a few days before the invasion fleet sailed, the equipment and men were loaded into the transports, and commissions issued to each man once safely at sea. On landing, with the beach head secured, the standard was set up as a symbol of intent. As supporters arrived they were enlisted, formed into files, issued weapons, assigned a company and NCO's selected. Finally, the companies were modelled into battalions, and within four days an army was formed; within 16 days they were ready to fight and beat a larger government army at the Battle of Norton St. Philip.

---

89 BL, Harley 6845, f.275.
90 John Erskine, *The Journal of the Hon. John Erskine of Carnock*, (Edinburgh:1893), p.120.
91 *Memoirs of William Veitch and George Brysson*, (Edinburgh: William Blackwood, 1825), p.326, 'every man of us had a halberd, besides special firelocks'.
92 T.B.Howell, *A Complete Collection of State Trials*, Volume 11, (London: Longman, 1816), p.1066.
93 Roger Morrice, *The Entring book of Roger Morrice*, Volume III, (Suffolk: Boydell & Brewer, 2007), p.19.

A battalion formed up in Battalia c.1685. Authors collection

Whig Armies of 1685 are the perfect study of how seventeenth century armies are formed and demonstrate the importance of logistics. By understanding the modelling and planning before the invasion, Monmouth's and Argyll's men are turned from the romantic 'pitchfork army' of popular non-fiction, into a fledgling professional army. With all this in place, it is now possible to imagine the scene on June 22, as five regiments of foot were arrayed on Sydenham Mead, near Keynsham. Each had six companies, each with a stand of pike in the centre behind the five regimental colours. On the wings of each pike block were divisions of musketeers and to the right, was a company of mixed scythes. On each flank of the army were six or seven squadrons of horse, with each trooper armed with pistols and a sword. Behind the Duke of Monmouth were three troops of cavalry, with each man in back and breast, and armed with a quad-barrelled pistol and a doubled-barrelled carbine. This squadron sat under a golden cornet, with a lace fringe upon which are the initials J.R. and a Crown. Alongside the Duke was a company of scythe men with a dark green standard with the motto 'Fear Nothing but God' emblazoned in gold. With most of the officers and some of the soldiers wearing purple coats faced with red, the picture was complete. Monmouth's Army became the fighting force akin to the Royalists at Edgehill.

Table 1: Equipment Seized in 1684[1]

546	Musquetts
3	Do. With Wheel Locks
247	Snaph Musqtts.
60	Matchlock Musqtts.
14	Musquettoons
4	Bullet Guns
1	Great Guns
122	Long Guns or ffowling pces.
364	Birding peeces
1	Double Barrll. Gun
54	Carbines
4	Do. Wth. Wheel Locks
20	Blunderbusses
9	Ditto. Brass
2	Ditto. Iron
3	Petronells
238 pr.	Pistols
40 pr.	Pistls wth. Wheel Locks
1	Pockett Pistolls
2	Cross Bowes
1	Rack for dto.
Color. 232	Bandaleers
33	Musqtt. Rests
1	Cartouch Box
6	Spanners
7	Sweads ffeathers
3 1/2 lb. & 2 barrlls.	Powder
3.2.14	Match
2 pr.	Bullet Moulds
1 bag	Bullets
102	Halberls
10	Partizans

1 NA, WO 55/1760.

3	Javelins
2	Colour Staffs
127	Pikes
41	Halfe (or Short) Pikes
28	Sherifs Javelins
23	Black (or Watch) Bills
11	Forrest Bills
8	Clubbs wth. Spikes
1	Danish Clubb
3	Pole-axes
1	Battle axe
1	Watch Staff
416	Swords
169	Swords Rapiers &c.
138	Rapiers
29	Hangers or Cutlaces
5	Tucks
1	Dagger

Table 2: Weapons Seized at Bridgwater in 1684[2]

Number	Weapon
15	Muskets
10	Pikes
4	Half Pikes
32	Swords
17	Fowling Pieces

2   NA, WO 55/1760.

Table 3: One of Argyll's Manifests[3]

Quantity	Measure & Item
20,000	lb gunpowder
9,000	lb saltpetre
10,000	lb gunpowder
75,000	lb gunpowder
50,000	lb saltpetre
500	lb gunpowder
2	chests with Muskets
62,000	lb gunpowder
75	chests with Arms
12,000	lb bullets
45	chests with small arms
12,500	lb gunpowder
25,000	lb gunpowder
13,000	lb bullets
30	chests small arms
12	baskets main arms
12	baskets & sacks with pistol holsters
5	Cases with Trumpets
13	sacks with Drums
11,500	lb gunpowder
13,000	lb shot

Table 4: Wade's List[4]

1500	Foot Arms
1500	Cuirasses
4	Pieces of Artillery mounted on field carriages
200	Barrels of Powder
-	Small quantity of Grenado shells
-	Match and other things

3 BL, Add MS 41817, f.7.
4 BL, Harl, 6845, f.271r.

Table 5: Grey List[5]

1460	suites of Defensive Arms
100	muskets and bandoliers
500	Pikes
500	Swords
250	Barrels of powder
4	Small Field Pieces
	Small number of double barrelled carbines
	Small number of double barrelled pistols

[5] BL, Add MS 30077, f.28r.